THE SORROWS OF FREDERICK and HOLY GHOSTS

By Romulus Linney

Novels
HEATHEN VALLEY
SLOWLY, BY THY HAND UNFURLED

Plays
THE SORROWS OF FREDERICK
THE LOVE SUICIDE AT SCHOFIELD BARRACKS
DEMOCRACY
HOLY GHOSTS

THE SORROWS OF FREDERICK

ROMULUS LINNEY

and HOLY GHOSTS

An Original Harvest Book

Harcourt Brace Jovanovich

HBJ New York and London

Copyright © 1966, 1976, 1977 by Romulus Linney

All rights reserved. No part of this publication may be reproduced or transmitted in any form or by any means, electronic or mechanical, including photocopy, recording, or any information storage and retrieval system, without permission in writing from the publisher.

Printed in the United States of America

CAUTION: Professionals and amateurs are hereby warned that *The Sorrows of Frederick* and *Holy Ghosts*, being fully protected under the copyright laws of the United States of America, the British Empire, including the Dominion of Canada, and all other countries which are signatories to the Universal Copyright Convention and the International Copyright Union, are subject to royalty. All rights, including professional, amateur, motion picture, recitation, lecturing, public reading, radio broadcasting, and television, are strictly reserved. Particular emphasis is laid on the question of readings, permission for which must be secured from the author's agent in writing. Inquiries on professional rights (except for amateur rights) should be addressed to Mr. Gilbert Parker, Curtis Brown, Ltd., 575 Madison Avenue, New York, New York 10022; inquiries on translation rights should be addressed to Harcourt Brace Jovanovich, Inc., 757 Third Avenue, New York, New York 10017.

The amateur acting rights of *The Sorrows of Frederick* and *Holy Ghosts* are controlled exclusively by the Dramatists Play Service, Inc., 440 Park Avenue South, New York, New York 10016. No amateur performance of the play may be given without obtaining in advance the written permission of the Dramatists Play Service, Inc., and paying the requisite fee.

Picture credits are on page 186.

Library of Congress Cataloging in Publication Data

Linney, Romulus, 1930–
   The sorrows of Frederick and Holy ghosts.

   (An original harvest book ; HB 355)
   I. Linney, Romulus, 1930–   Holy ghosts. 1977. II. Title.
PS3562.I55S6   1977   812'.5'4   76-47904
ISBN 0-15-683848-6

First Original Harvest edition 1977

A B C D E F G H I J

The author wishes to thank the National Endowment for the Arts for its support during the writing of *Holy Ghosts*.

THE SORROWS OF FREDERICK

For Margaret Andrews Linney

Prologue

Most history is a compilation of lies, mixed with a few truths.
       Frederick the Great, in his *History of My Times*

Frederick II, called the Great, ruled Prussia for forty-six years, from 1740 until 1786. He had been a sensitive youth but he made a strong king.

The last time I saw him, at a review, he came riding his big white horse, wearing a plain blue coat, quite threadbare, the front covered with Spanish snuff. . . . Lurching forward in the saddle, he subjected his weary troops to a ferocious individual inspection.
       Latrobe, *Anecdotes of the Late King of Prussia*

A sad Creed, this of the King's; he had to do his duty without fee or reward. Yes, reader—and what is well worth your attention, you will have difficulty to find a King or a man who stood more faithfully to his duty. To poor Friedrich that was all the Law and all the Prophets.
       Carlyle, *History of Friedrich II of Prussia*

Nobody had the least suspicion that a tyrant of extraordinary military and political talents, of industry more extraordinary still, without fear, without faith, without mercy, had ascended the throne of Prussia. His selfish rapacity gave the signal to his neighbors. His example quieted their sense of shame. The whole world sprang to arms. On the head of Frederick is all the blood that was shed in a war that raged for many years.
       Macaulay, *Frederick the Great*

Prologue

Better be a eunuch in a Turkish harem than a Prussian subject.
Eighteenth-century proverb

Frederick came to the throne when Prussia was an insignificant part of the Holy Roman Empire. He attacked Austria at once, and annexed the large province of Silesia. Acting as his own general, he fought many fierce battles in the several Wars of the Austrian Succession.

With the first dawn of morning, the two armies, in close contact, rushed furiously upon each other. There were seventy thousand on the one side and seventy-five thousand on the other. They faced each other in straight lines over a plain nearly ten miles in length. It is vain to give the reader an adequate idea of the terrible battle which ensued. With musketry, artillery, gleaming sabres and rushing horsemen, the infuriate hosts dashed each upon the other. At length, the Austrians, having lost nine thousand dead and wounded, seven thousand prisoners, sixteen thousand in all, retreated, bleeding and exhausted. Frederick remained the undisputed victor of the field. Five thousand of his brave soldiers lay dead or wounded upon the plain. Such was the battle of Hohenfriedberg, once of world-wide renown, now almost forgotten.
Abbott, History of Frederick the Great

If you want an omelette, you must be prepared to break a few eggs.
Frederick, table talk

The same discipline that allowed him to drench Europe in blood without one word of consent from a single subject also allowed him to improve a legal code, build schools, drain and ditch and hedge his countryside. How splendid a figure, had his cause been just.
Lord Rosebery, Preface to de Catt's Frederick the Great

Frederick won his wars to keep Silesia. He found himself famous. He was a statesman, a general, a lawmaker, but also a philosopher, an historian, a fine flutist, a composer, and a poet. He built a beautiful retreat, named it Sans Souci, and held elegant dinner parties there, receiving many famous visitors.

He rises at five in summer, six in winter. After a simple breakfast he plays the flute and thinks about philosophy and affairs of state. In the mornings he drills his troops. At noon, his meal is accompanied by conferences, and then matters of administration are very speedily accomplished. In the early evenings he will often attend or play in a concert with his musicians, scientists, poets and artists. At eight-thirty he has supper with his distinguished friends.

Thomas Campbell, *Frederick the Great*

Pee well and be cheerful; it's the best we can do on this earth. My hemorrhoids salute your gonorrhea. Frederick, to a friend

His most famous visitor was Voltaire.

You are, perhaps, the greatest king who ever lived. Voltaire

I was born too soon, but I have no regrets. I have known Voltaire. Frederick

He always talks like a philosopher just before he acts like a king. Voltaire

You make the mind laugh, and the soul weep. Frederick

You keep threatening suicide. How can you pretend to live as a philosopher, if you can't live as a man? Voltaire

He is a chaos of clear ideas. Frederick

Frederick was threatened by a coalition of Austria, Russia, and France, who were determined to make him give up Silesia and to destroy the new Prussia that was upsetting the balances of power. Frederick attacked first, and plunged Europe into the Seven Years' War.

Waves of blood are washing over the world, and the source

Act I

FREDERSDORF
> Yes, Majesty.

KATTE
> Yes, Majesty.

FREDERICK WILLIAM
> Your attendants are satisfactory, Prince. As they will now make reports to me, I'll permit them to attend you, closely. Fredersdorf, more to drink for His Royal Highness.
>
> [FREDERSDORF *takes another tankard to the Prince, who drinks.*]
>
> Don't sip, damn it, drink! Doesn't drink, doesn't hunt. Hides in a thicket and reads a book. At least he doesn't walk on tiptoe anymore. Got over that, somehow.
>
> [*The* CHANCELLOR, *drunk, crosses the line.*]

CHANCELLOR
> But, Sire, we must be fair. We all understand he acquitted himself like a man in the harems of the King of Poland, on your recent journey to Dresden.
>
> [*Everybody senses danger. The* CHANCELLOR *blunders on.*]
>
> And there are, so one hears, current and delightful afternoons in Berlin with flutes and a fetching young lady, named Ritter.

FREDERICK WILLIAM
> I didn't hear anything about that.

CHANCELLOR
> Own up, Your Royal Highness! The Presentor's daughter? Duets in the afternoons while her father's away? I know it for a fact. You see, Sire, we have a stirring of the manly instinct after all! [*He laughs, sees the ugly stare on the King's face, turns pale.*]

FREDERICK WILLIAM
Nobody told me. Fritz?

[*No answer*]

Fritz!

FREDERICK
Rumors, Papa. To make you angry with me. Rumors.

FREDERICK WILLIAM
We will see. I'll have that Ritter girl examined, Prince. God help her if there's not a smooth plug in that hole. And even if there is, if the little bitch has tried to corrupt you, she'll be whipped in the streets. Will you be debauched into a fool with his brains in his britches? [*To the* CHANCELLOR] And you, sir! Note carefully this is not the court of France! We are not lewd, we do not pander! Such creatures cannot fight, they lose all decency, strength, and honor. We are a poor thing, not elegant, and no diplomat, but we know our honor! [*Drunk, he stands and shouts.*] I contain my lust! In all my long years of marriage, gentlemen, I never once betrayed my vows! [*He strikes the table a tremendous blow.*] Never once! Show me another king in Europe who can say that! [FREDERICK WILLIAM *takes a deep drink and spills beer down his chin onto his chest. He wipes his coat with his hand. He looks up to see his son staring at him with disgust.*] What are *you* looking at?

[*The Prince puts down his tankard and stands up.*]

FREDERICK [*quietly*]
I shall look where I please.

[*Panic. The* CABINET *is terrified.*]

FREDERICK WILLIAM
What? What did he say?

Prologue

of much of it is Frederick the Great. He came to the throne with a shrivelled heart and a sardonic scorn for all mankind: its morals, its conventions, its cant. There was little human left.
Lord Rosebery

Impressions one receives in childhood cannot be erased from the soul.
Frederick

He won, and again kept Silesia, but the price he paid was enormous, both in his own health and well-being, and in the lives and properties of his people. He worked hard to rebuild his nation.

He interfered with everything. We can make shift to live under a debauchee or a tyrant, but to be ruled by a busybody is more than human nature can bear.
Macaulay

Blessed are the absent, for they know not what is happening.
Frederick

In his last years he held intensive Army maneuvers and continually inspected his kingdom. He withdrew from other people.

I am tired of ruling a nation of slaves.
Frederick

Inarticulate notions, fancies, transient aspirations, he might have, in the background of his mind. One day, sitting for a while out of doors, gazing into the Sun, he was heard to murmur, "Perhaps I will be nearer thee soon"; and indeed, nobody knows who he meant or what his thoughts were in those final months. There is traceable only a complete superiority to Fear and Hope; in parts, too, are half-glimpses of a great motionless interior lake of Sorrow, sadder than any tears or complaining, which are altogether wanting to it.
Carlyle

Characters

The King
FREDERICK II OF PRUSSIA, *called the Great*

His Family
FREDERICK WILLIAM I, *his father*
ELIZABETH CHRISTINE, *his wife*

His Cabinet
THE GENERAL
THE DOCTOR
THE CHANCELLOR
THE BISHOP

His Friends
LIEUTENANT NOCKLIN-GRANTZ / LIEUTENANT HANS KATTE / LIEUTENANT KORT
A PRIVATE SOLDIER / M. G. FREDERSDORF
VOLTAIRE

His Soldiers
SOLDIER 1
SOLDIER 2
THE EXECUTIONER / THE POTSDAM GIANT

PLACE: *Prussia*
TIME: *1712–1786*

ACT I
The Prince

At rear are low platforms and ramps. We hear a ghostly subject played on a flute: the opening notes of Bach's Musical Offering, a theme given him by FREDERICK. *Light reveals an old man, eyes closed, propped up on an iron cot. He breathes with difficulty and sighs in his sleep. At his feet lie a faded blue Prussian uniform coat, a three-cornered hat, boots, and a cane.*

Enter SOLDIER 1, *with a watch. He comes to attention with a sharp crack of his boots.*

SOLDIER 1
Majesty! Five o'clock!

[FREDERICK *wakes, nods.* SOLDIER 1 *puts papers on his cot beside him, exits. Enter* SOLDIER 2 *with a basin of water and a towel.* FREDERICK *dabs a few drops of water on his face, coughs, and spits. Exit* SOLDIER 2. *Enter* SOLDIER 1 *carrying a tray with coffee and one piece of bread.* FREDERICK *eats, studies papers, has his boots put on.*]

FREDERICK
Are they all here?

SOLDIER 1
Yes, Majesty.

FREDERICK
All right. The General and the Lieutenant.

[*Exit* SOLDIER 1. FREDERICK *puts a wig on his head and gets into his uniform coat. He is a strange, shabby figure, consumed, when he is alone, by sadness. Enter the* GEN-

ERAL *and* LIEUTENANT NOCKLIN-GRANTZ, *smartly, in step. They stand before him in dazzling Prussian uniforms.*]

FREDERICK
Well, gentlemen?

GENERAL
Sire, Baron Heinrich Nocklin-Grantz has the honor to present his son, Lieutenant in Your Majesty's Death's Head Hussars. The Baron has asked me to speak for his progress as an officer, in view of his proposed marriage to the oldest daughter of the house of Larnbach.

FREDERICK
And do you, General?

GENERAL
Majesty, while I firmly uphold the tradition of celibacy among the Death's Head Hussars, I also present my unqualified approval of this young man's performance of his duties.

FREDERICK
And what does that mean?

GENERAL
Why, that I heartily approve of his achievements as an officer.

FREDERICK
So. Grantz-Larnbach. Fat dowry, adjoining estates. Perfection, except for the trifling obstacle of the Hussars. Well, how's the girl? Bearable, young man?

LIEUTENANT NOCKLIN-GRANTZ
Yes, Majesty.

FREDERICK
Wonderful. Now what, General? A transfer from the Hussars?

Act I

GENERAL

I would heartily approve that, Sire.

FREDERICK [*sharply*]

Yes, but do you propose it?

GENERAL

Majesty, if Your Majesty declares himself in favor of this matter, then I hope it may be so; if not, why, then, Your Majesty doubtless knows what he is about.

FREDERICK

Thank you. Gentlemen, we need brave officers, not fat estates. Young man, allow me to instruct you, your nervous commanding officer, and your distinguished father: A Prussian Hussar does not seek his fortune through the vagina, but by the sword! Your request is denied. I bid you both good morning.

[*They salute and leave.* FREDERICK *studies another paper. Enter* SOLDIER 1.]

Doctor!

[*Exit* SOLDIER 1. FREDERICK *takes a jeweled snuffbox from his pocket, jams snuff into his nose, sneezes violently, wipes his nose with his hand, and his hand on his coat. Enter the* DOCTOR.]

Well, sir, you come in a long and honorable tradition. One more doctor to try and keep this old man alive. Let me tell you that he suffers from dropsy, gout, and a moldering disposition. Campfires blaze all day in his chest, and last night he took three cups of blood from God knows how many hemorrhoids. What do you think?

DOCTOR

I think I see before me a stout-hearted old man whose spirit seems healthy. It often rules the body, Sire.

FREDERICK

A healthy spirit! You don't know what you are talking about. Here you are, come from medical college, with your pockets no doubt filled with stomachs, scrotums, and lungs, to treat me. But what, really, do you know about suffering, Doctor? How many graves have you filled?

DOCTOR [*coolly*]

Not so many as Your Majesty.

FREDERICK

Well, I see you have a healthy spirit, anyway. What part of an old king would you bleed to save a new nation?

DOCTOR

The heart. But that is fatal.

FREDERICK

My dear Doctor, what a shame you didn't go into the Army. It would be a pleasure to have you about in the field. Now, can you keep me from constipating myself with eel pie, and eating too many spices, dangerous passions in the strict days of old age?

DOCTOR

No, Majesty.

FREDERICK

Oh?

DOCTOR

I cannot overcome the nature of the King of Prussia. But when he collapses, I will get him on his feet again.

FREDERICK

Then you have your appointment! Good morning!

[*Exit the* DOCTOR. *Enter* SOLDIER 1.]

Chancellor!

Act I

[*Exit* SOLDIER 1. *Enter the* CHANCELLOR.]

Good morning. I have investigated your monthly depositions and I have approved three verdicts against five of your district administrations. You were all wrong about that tax proclamation in Magdeburg. Two of your acreage allotments are incorrect. You are wrong about the depth of the wine barrels in Küstrin, and about the new method of shearing sheep. Well?

CHANCELLOR

I cannot defend myself. I did the best I could.

FREDERICK

I know that. Please stop shaking. I'm not going to shoot you. The rest of your effort seems capable, only lacking in detail. I require full particulars, always! I have corrected part of your deposition. Here! [FREDERICK *peers over the* CHANCELLOR's *shoulder as he studies the paper.*] Do you see? Here! And here!

CHANCELLOR

Yes, yes, Majesty. That is the way it should be done.

FREDERICK

Then *do* it that way! Good morning!

[*Exit the* CHANCELLOR. *Enter* SOLDIER 1.]

Bishop!

[*Exit* SOLDIER 1. *Enter the* BISHOP.]

[*With great charm*] I am delighted to see you, my dear friend. My apologies for this miserable hour, but I have to fight today and we must chat a bit first. You are looking extremely well.

BISHOP

I am very happy to see Your Majesty.

FREDERICK

Good. Well, the Holy Ghost and I have agreed that the prelate Fuhlweisse will be coadjutor of Breslau. We have mutually decided that you and all your brothers in Christ who oppose him will be looked upon as offering blasphemous resistance to the Holy Ghost.

BISHOP

This great understanding between Your Majesty and the Holy Ghost is something new—I did not know that you were even acquainted with him. Fuhlweisse is not acceptable.

FREDERICK

You have always been more sensible than your scheming brothers in Christ. Come now, relent.

[*No response*]

You know, I envy the heavenly Jerusalem you win for yourself. I will doubtless not qualify. My nature has become sour here in the backwaters of age and responsibility. I would surely make an impossible angel.

[*No response*]

On the other hand, I insist about Fuhlweisse, and I do not shake with fear at holy displeasure, as my father did.

BISHOP

Majesty, you are a thousand times greater than your father, God rest him. But Fuhlweisse is not acceptable.

FREDERICK

You are about to cause yourself a great deal of trouble. I promise that Fuhlweisse will have nothing to say about the Church. He will only deal with civil authorities. If he gets out of hand, martyr him.

Act I

BISHOP

He is not acceptable.

FREDERICK

Then I will martyr you. Re-read your sacred history. It is not difficult. I can have your ring tomorrow and give it to my dogs to sharpen their teeth on. Come now, in the name of a reasonable God, I support the Church like a timid monk, you let me have Fuhlweisse where I want him.

BISHOP

Do you really believe I serve the Church with scorn? That I don't understand how Your Majesty's tolerance is nothing but his contempt? I have my faith. I put my trust in God. Fuhlweisse is not acceptable. Martyr us both, if you can.

FREDERICK

I'll do my best. Good morning!

[*The* BISHOP *turns to leave.*]

One moment!

BISHOP

Yes?

FREDERICK

We are both very old. We should manage these things better, really. Everyone knows that at the eleventh hour I will crack my whip and you will jump. Can't you at least drop the pretense that you have any *faith* to fight about?

BISHOP

It is not a pretense, Sire.

FREDERICK

Can't do it, can you? You just can't do it. Will you then

still maintain with me that the soul and the body are two separate commodities? Come now, do you insist on surviving your earthly destruction?

BISHOP
I do.

FREDERICK
How?

BISHOP
By memory. Does not the King remember the faith of the Prince?

FREDERICK
No.

BISHOP
I beg Your Majesty to try.

FREDERICK
Absurd! You would define religious faith as something remembered? Something recalled from youth, like a boy's vision of love?

BISHOP
Exactly. It has to be, at our age.

[*Exit the* BISHOP. FREDERICK *stares after him.*]

FREDERICK [*aloud*]
The soul and the body two things? An immortal soul, that lives on and on, after the body has perished? Ridiculous! Thank God!

[*Enter* SOLDIER 1.]

Court-martial. The accused and the General.

[*Exit* SOLDIER 1. FREDERICK *studies his papers. Enter the* GENERAL *and the* PRIVATE SOLDIER. *The* PRIVATE SOLDIER *is very short, a stocky peasant standing barely five feet tall.*

Act I   15

He is slow-witted, but he holds himself straight, ready to accept his fate.]

I am interested in this man, General. Please bear with me. Name?

PRIVATE SOLDIER
Johan Fredersdorf, Great Eternal Majesty.

FREDERICK
"Majesty" is enough, never mind the stuffing. Are you from Silesia?

PRIVATE SOLDIER
No, Majesty.

FREDERICK
Then you are no relation to an old man named Michael Gabriel Fredersdorf?

PRIVATE SOLDIER
No, Majesty.

FREDERICK
I am sorry to hear it. He looked just like you. Same size, everything. He was a great friend, when I was young and needed one. Dead now. Fredersdorf, poor old thing. My God, how I miss him.

[FREDERICK *begins to weep openly. The* GENERAL *stares at him.*]

[*Crying*] How good he was! What a fine man he was! Don't distress yourself, General, I weep, but I win! Oh, but really, really, you both should have known him. Fredersdorf, oh, Fredersdorf!

PRIVATE SOLDIER
Yes, Majesty?

[FREDERICK *stares at him, laughs violently, wipes his eyes.*]

FREDERICK
> Oh, not you, for God's sake! Well, well, court-martial. Something we can't cry away or laugh away. Is it, gentlemen?

PRIVATE SOLDIER
> No, Majesty!

GENERAL
> No, Majesty!

FREDERICK
> I'm glad we all agree. You were the President of the Court, General. Correct?

GENERAL
> It is, Sire.

FREDERICK
> And you approve this verdict?

GENERAL
> Without hesitation!

FREDERICK
> I see. Well, soldier, you have been sentenced to death by hanging for having sexual relations with your horse. [*Pause*] Did you have sexual relations with your horse?

PRIVATE SOLDIER
> Yes, Majesty.

FREDERICK
> A mare, I hope?

PRIVATE SOLDIER
> Yes, Majesty.

FREDERICK
> Still, it's shocking. [*He peers at the* PRIVATE SOLDIER.] Tell me, what did you stand on?

Act I

PRIVATE SOLDIER
A bucket, Eternal Majesty. It fell over.

FREDERICK
The bucket or the horse?

PRIVATE SOLDIER
The bucket.

FREDERICK
Harrowing. Nevertheless, you have been condemned to death because of it. Do you know any reason why I should change that?

[*The* PRIVATE SOLDIER *stares stupidly at the King. He sinks to his knees.* FREDERICK *writes on the court-martial papers and hands them to the* GENERAL.]

Verdict!

GENERAL [*reads*]
"Pardoned. Transferred to the Infantry."

PRIVATE SOLDIER [*scrambles to his feet*]
Thank you, thank you, Great Eternal Majesty!

FREDERICK
I am only sorry you must lose your horse.

[*Exit* PRIVATE SOLDIER.]

All right, General. I can guess your thoughts. What would have happened had his name been Schmidt?

GENERAL
He'd have been shot.

FREDERICK
I'm glad you have a logical mind. Now, be so good as to relax a moment. Please sit on my cot. Thank you. Please don't sulk. Thank you. [FREDERICK *studies the* GENERAL, *who sits stiffly, outraged at such treatment.*] This is your

first field command with me. We all know your reputation from Spain and France. You are a famous warrior. But you were all fudge and pasty pudding about that marriage, and then you decide the dreadful fate of a blockheaded soldier with his brains in his britches, condemn him to death without hesitation. You were vague when you should have been decisive, and decisive when you should have been vague. I hope you don't fight the way you think. Now then, anything you would like to know before we review the Army?

GENERAL
As a matter of fact, there is! Where, Majesty, are we going to meet the enemy?

FREDERICK
Can you keep a secret?

GENERAL
Of course.

FREDERICK
So can I. [*He laughs.*] Agreed?

[*The* GENERAL *rises, very much insulted.*]

GENERAL
As Your Majesty desires.

FREDERICK
Man, you are stiff as a poker. We aren't getting along too well, you and I. You're not very good at small talk, General.

GENERAL
Perhaps that is because there is an Army arrayed outside, waiting for me to lead it into battle.

FREDERICK
Possibly. But that Army out there is the Army of Prussia,

Act I

and it is waiting for me, not for you. My father created it, I perfected it. Now, I know you are going to earn your enormous salary, but please realize the limits of your commission. They'll wait, don't you think?

GENERAL
Certainly, Sire.

FREDERICK
Yes. Now, as long as we are being so intimate, have I ever shown you this? [*He takes a gilded snuffbox from his coat.*]

GENERAL
Exquisite. A beautiful thing.

FREDERICK
Notice the black ivory, and the jeweled hinges. This is the way it opens. Snuff?

GENERAL
Thank you, no.

FREDERICK
Do you know what it is?

GENERAL
I have heard it is opium.

FREDERICK
Just enough to kill me. An oval of gold and eighteen little pills, and they ease my wretched mind so much, so much. But some less lethal snuff, surely we need it. Here!

[*He takes out another snuffbox. They pinch, salute each other, put snuff in their nostrils, and sneeze, the* GENERAL *with careful delicacy,* FREDERICK *with appalling sloppiness, wiping his coat with his hand.*]

GENERAL [*making a face*]
Ah! Good! Very good!

FREDERICK [*making a face*]
   My father tried to hang me once, when I was a child. He did it behind a large velvet curtain, with a sash. My mother cut me down. When I take snuff, and sneeze, the relief is like that. Like being unhung, if you follow me.

GENERAL
   Indeed, yes, Majesty.

FREDERICK
   Indeed, no, General. What do you know about it? You were not the bullied child set out on a parade ground at the age of three! [*He holds up first one snuffbox and then the other.*] One to ease my body, and another to ease my mind. If there is no heaven, at least here is final peace and permanence. How I long for that. [*He strikes a pose and declaims:*]

   > O Germans! Your intestinal wars and your broils,
   > The frenzies of your wraths clutch you in their toils!

   [*He looks at the amazed* GENERAL *and laughs.*] Well, not so good as Voltaire, no, but then, Voltaire never composed verses on the morning of a fight, did he? Poetry, General, and a pillbox of deadly opium. That's the way I lull the poor child within me, keep him from crying, and send him to war and sleep. [*Suddenly, explosively*] Children should not be punished, General! Remember that! They will learn consequence without punishment! They will! Do you believe that?

GENERAL
   Certainly, Sire.

FREDERICK
   Do you beat your children?

GENERAL
   I have none.

Act I

FREDERICK
Oh. Well, God knows that's not the answer. All right, then. [*He takes up his cane and his hat.*] Have they learned to play my march yet?

GENERAL
Yes, Majesty.

FREDERICK
How do you like it?

GENERAL
It is absolute perfection, Sire.

FREDERICK
All right, all right.

[*The* GENERAL *salutes and leaves.* FREDERICK *stands, thinking.*]

Let me see. Now, let me see.

> The ox must plow the furrow,
> The nightingale sing afar,
> The dolphin swim, O innocence,
> And I—I must make war!

[FREDERICK's *Hohenfriedburg "Victory March" is heard, played by a strident military band.*]

Not bad. On the morning of a fight, that's not so bad.

[*He turns, faces upstage, and stands waiting, leaning on his cane. A high platform rolls forward.* FREDERICK *climbs its steps to address the Prussian Army. This platform can be built into the shape of a huge wooden horse—a grotesque shambles of a horse, split, splintered, held up by braces and props, as if it were a gigantic child's hobby-horse grown up to a terrible old age.* FREDERICK *can mount, hauling himself up into its saddle, to give his battle speech from horseback.*]

Soldiers! You stand now where your fathers stood, once more to follow your queer and upstart old King into battle. Let me tell you something about the commanding General of the Army we are going to demolish. He is a clotheshorse. His wardrobe fills four rooms. He owns, believe me, one thousand five hundred wigs. He would be the absolute delight of all the empresses who surrounded us years ago, when we were nothing. They are no longer with us, poor ladies, but if they were, they would certainly count on this gentleman to deliver us up to them, hacked apart with his perfumed hands. Look at our enemies with me. The world sees glitter and power. What do I see? Yesterday, a closetful of whores, today a prancing clotheshorse! One thousand five hundred wigs, but no head! Well, soldiers, are we women in Prussia? Are we tiny tots with curling hair and pink toes? Are we the wood from which frightened children, bashful boys, and milksop husbands are carved? Or are we the sons of our fathers? Soldiers?

[*Drum roll*]

Now, let me see bright sunlight on Austrian rumps! Show me bayonets! Into their lungs! Up their noses! Give me their ribs and their bellies and the shreds of their fat Austrian assholes! Follow your King and save our nation! Which of you would live forever? Soldiers?

[*Cannonade. A roar of soldiers. The crashing chords of the "Victory March." Sounds of soldiers marching. Enter* SOLDIER 2. *He holds up a pouch.* FREDERICK *takes the pouch, opens it, takes out a letter, tosses the pouch to* SOLDIER 2, *who catches it and kneels.* FREDERICK *tears open the letter and reads it quickly. The roar of the soldiers, the cannonades, the "Victory March," all reach a chaotic climax.* FREDERICK *holds one thin arm up into the air. Everything stops.*]

Act I

[*Very quietly, to* SOLDIER 2.] Tell them I will be there tomorrow night. I want to see the body. Have everything prepared. Don't stop to breathe. I'll be right behind you. Fly.

[*Exit* SOLDIER 2.]

General.

[*Enter the* GENERAL.]

Call them back.

GENERAL
   What?

FREDERICK
   Call back the Army. Make camp and fortify it. We will not attack today.

GENERAL [*shocked*]
   That's impossible! Majesty, the enemy is in sight! We have no choice! We must attack! Now!

[FREDERICK *weeps*.]

   I must inform Your Majesty that if we do not attack now as planned, I must resign my commission. I have never in all my career deserted a battlefield!

FREDERICK [*crying*]
   I won't lose your battle, General.

GENERAL [*disgusted*]
   Well, win it then. [*He turns on his heel and walks away.*]

FREDERICK
   Come back here, you pig!

[*Amazed, the* GENERAL *turns and stares.* FREDERICK *comes down from his platform or dismounts from his horse.*]

Forgive me, forgive me. You see me like a dog, biting

into a stone. My whole life, General, is a battlefield, and I have just received a wound. I forget how to treat my officers, who are loyal and brave, as you are. Accept my apologies and bear with me.

GENERAL
Then what shall we do, Sire?

FREDERICK
Encamp the Army. Boldly. Parade a battalion about. The Austrians will spend a week wondering what we are up to. They won't attack, I know them. Listen, General. How many times this same thing has happened to me! It's my curse. My sister, my brother, my mother, Fredersdorf, Voltaire, all died as I marched about victorious, and the news always came to me at moments of triumph. That's how *that* works. My casualties are those I love the most. I thought it was over, finished. There was no one left for me to mourn, but there is, there is! It has come upon me again. Oh, God!

GENERAL
Your Majesty, what has happened? Who has been lost?

FREDERICK
We try to save them by saying everything is eternal, but it is all finished at death. I am an old man, sick at heart. God knows I have the right to be. Stop fretting, General, about your military reputation. I will come back soon enough and polish it for you.

GENERAL
You are leaving?

FREDERICK
Do you mind?

GENERAL
Majesty.

Act I

FREDERICK
> Encamp the Army. I leave it in your hands, God help me. Be good enough to have it here when I return. Fire one shot without me and I will hang you up by your balls! Oh, I don't mean to insult you, sir, forgive me. It's difficult for you to understand an old wretch like me. Generals are very brave, but so limited. Oh, where is Fredersdorf? And Voltaire, that monkey! They would know what is killing me!

GENERAL
> I am grieved to see Your Majesty so distressed.

FREDERICK
> Ah, this damned letter! Why did I live to receive it? Why not just one little lead bullet, here, into the brain of the King? Ludicrous! Ridiculous! All right. I will leave, for home, now. I will return in two days, at most. Everyone will think it strategy of the most sublime brilliance. The truth, General? Well, an old man is going home to attend the funeral of his dog. [*Pause*] What do you think about that?

GENERAL [*beyond amazement*]
> I follow Your Majesty's orders. [*Exit the* GENERAL.]

FREDERICK [*holding up the letter*]
> For this, I will desert the field! [*He climbs on his horse or platform, which moves.*] O grief! Mount up behind me, and gallop home with me! What infernal company! [*Exit* FREDERICK.]

[*Blackout. Drums, in the rhythm of a galloping horse. Perhaps we see a vague shadow moving, resembling an old man riding a horse not only across a countryside but also into the past. Music and the drums make us aware of a change in time, back to the birth and childhood of the King. Enter the* CABINET.]

CHANCELLOR

The Prince of Prussia shall be raised to manhood with the utmost care.

DOCTOR

His little hands, when they can grasp, will hold drums and small weapons.

BISHOP

His legs will be wrapped in strong leather boots.

GENERAL

His voice will learn the commands of the field.

CHANCELLOR

His eyes will see into the joints and bulwarks of the State.

DOCTOR

His body will suffer the obligations of a child who must one day rule a kingdom.

BISHOP

His mind will embrace the dutiful worship of Almighty God.

GENERAL

The Prince will be up, dressed, and ready for the tasks before him from the instant he opens his eyes. He will consume his breakfast in three minutes. He will organize his person in four, and take up his duties in one. From bed to parade ground, not one second more than a quarter of an hour.

[*Exit the* CABINET. *Flute music, a passage of time. Enter* M. G. FREDERSDORF *and* LIEUTENANT HANS KATTE. *They listen. Applause. Enter* FREDERICK *as a sixteen-year-old prince, with his flute.*]

FREDERICK [*violently excited*]

The truth! Tell the truth now, both of you. What was it like?

Act I

KATTE
> You heard the applause.

FREDERICK
> Katte, you imbecile, that's not the truth. Anyone will applaud a prince. Now listen, I'm serious. What did you think? You first, Fredersdorf.

FREDERSDORF
> What can I ever tell you about your music? I thought it was very nice. It made me think about the wind at night. I don't know what else to say.

FREDERICK
> Katte?

KATTE
> It was very beautiful.

FREDERICK
> Flattery! If you really mean what you say, Katte, you'll remember this: How many times did my first theme repeat? Were you really listening? How many times?

KATTE [*after thinking*]
> Four! Yes four!

FREDERICK [*embracing him fiercely*]
> Oh, you do mean what you say! You do! Forgive me!

KATTE
> Never mind that. You just composed a beautiful sonata. You ought to be proud of yourself.

FREDERICK
> Oh, it's more than that. How can I tell you what it means to have music come out of me. I would rather spend my life with this frail thing than rule a universe of kingdoms. My God, it's enough just to listen, but when that music comes from me, Katte, Fredersdorf, I want to die with joy. Does that embarrass you? Does that seem so absurd?

KATTE
> Not to me.

FREDERSDORF
> It does to me. That is because I am one thing and you are another.

FREDERICK
> Good old Fredersdorf. It's pure desire. That's all. Fredersdorf, there's nothing more wonderful than desire.

FREDERSDORF
> And nothing more dangerous.

FREDERICK
> Oh, I don't care! Pure, simple desire! That's all I am! I am nothing else *but* desire! I am a prince, and I know how to sing, and I want to dance and shout and—God help me! my friends—conceive beautiful things.

FREDERSDORF
> Then, that is what you must do.

KATTE
> And so you will. You have already begun.

FREDERICK
> Yes, yes, but sometimes my desire, it's, well . . . well, I feel as if it will choke me to death. Katte, I have finished my comedy, did I tell you?

KATTE
> No, I am delighted. When can I read it?

FREDERICK
> Tonight. And then, more surprises, there's this! A letter. Looks quite ordinary. Paper, ink. But who wrote it? Look, Fredersdorf!

FREDERSDORF
> Is he a good man? I hope so.

Act I

FREDERICK
>Give it to Katte.

KATTE
>Wonderful! Wonderful!

FREDERICK
>Who do you think he is, Fredersdorf? Come on, guess!

FREDERSDORF
>Stop teasing. Tell me or don't.

FREDERICK
>Katte, read the end!

KATTE [*reads*]
>"You are a prince certain to be beloved of mankind. For you sing like Orpheus, you think like Aristotle, and you write like Pindar. A philosophical prince, who will make men happy, fills me with admiration. You are the hope of mankind. [*Pause*] Voltaire."

FREDERICK
>Voltaire! The greatest writer in the world, Fredersdorf, and the only fearless man in Europe! And he writes me this letter. He's willing to come and visit me! Voltaire visit me. I'll admit I wrote him first, and laid it on a bit. But the hope of mankind? My God!

FREDERSDORF
>Then, he is a good man. You are.

FREDERICK
>No, that's silly. But I would like to be. Great rulers are said to be men of action, born that way, who get things done. I know they are overpraised mediocrities chosen by luck. Everything good I possess—my philosophy, my music, my poetry—I had to steal. I won them by strategy and deception. Nothing was given me. I will be a different

king with a different arsenal than those who have gone before me. I will.

KATTE [*softly*]
Bravo, Majesty.

[*Enter the* GENERAL. *He salutes* FREDERICK *coldly.*]

FREDERICK
Yes?

GENERAL
Your father, the King of Prussia, is waiting for you, Your Royal Highness.

FREDERICK
Is he? Oh yes. Well, all right. Tell him I'm coming.

[*Exit the* GENERAL.]

Fredersdorf! Katte! Come with me!

[*Exeunt* KATTE, FREDERSDORF, *and* FREDERICK. *A voice bellows drill commands. Enter the* POTSDAM GIANT, *a Prussian soldier seven feet tall, going through a manual of arms. Soldiers bring on a rough wooden table holding large beer mugs, clay pipes, and wooden seats. This is the King's smoking room, his "Tobacco Parliament." Enter* FREDERICK WILLIAM I *and his* CABINET. *They all clap in unison with the executed movements of the* POTSDAM GIANT. *They finish with him, shouting.*]

ALL
One, two, three, four!

[FREDERICK WILLIAM *seizes his giant, pounds him on the back with ferocious glee.*]

FREDERICK WILLIAM
Wonderful! Wonderful! That is the way *that* should be done!

Act I

[*The* POTSDAM GIANT *stands to one side, at attention.* FREDERICK WILLIAM *and his* CABINET *take up their beer and tobacco.*]

Now, gentlemen, we have a very important artistic event scheduled for this evening. But we need His Royal Highness. [*He drinks deeply, looks around, and scowls.*] Where in hell is Fritz?

[*Enter* FREDERICK, KATTE, *and* FREDERSDORF.]

FREDERICK
Here, Majesty.

FREDERICK WILLIAM
Come and go when you please, do you? No respect for my schedule? Who's that with you?

FREDERICK
My valet, Fredersdorf. My friend, Lieutenant Hans Katte. I ask Your Majesty to allow them to attend me this evening.

FREDERICK WILLIAM
Attendants, is it? [*Grandly*] Very well. Your father is always ready to show proper respect, which is a damn sight more than he gets from you. [*To the* GENERAL] Tell them they may *stand* attendant upon His Royal Highness, and escort His Royal Highness to his chair.

[*The* GENERAL *escorts* FREDERICK *to a straight-backed chair with hare's ears stuck on it. He blushes, but sits. The* CABINET *laughs.*]

All right. Now that we're all together, where is our artistic event? [*Shouting*] Bring it in! [*To the* CABINET] And somebody give His Royal Highness something to drink, to get the starch out of him.

[*A huge tankard of beer is given to* FREDERICK. *Enter* SOLDIER 2 *with a covered canvas.*]

A toast to His Royal Highness! Drink it down, monkey!

CABINET [*on their feet, toasting loudly*]
To His Royal Highness!

FREDERICK WILLIAM
Not so quick, not so quick, gentlemen! He's not the King yet! If he keeps prancing about the way he does, he never will be. [*To* FREDERICK] All, Prince! Drink it all!

[FREDERICK *struggles, and manages to down his drink.* FREDERICK WILLIAM *motions, and another is immediately brought to him.*]

Now, then! As all the world knows, we have in our kingdom an artistic prince. He plays the flute. He writes verses. He corresponds with French authors. Very well. But what about the King? Does he have *his* artistic side, too? He does. He dabs a little paint, he does! He is not entirely ignorant of the world of Art! So, in honor of the Prince, the latest opus of the King!! Let's see it!

[SOLDIER 2 *unveils the painting. It is a portrait of a monkey in fancy court dress.* FREDERICK WILLIAM *laughs. The* CABINET *laughs.*]

Bravo! Bravo! Now, *that's* good work! Very sensitive, very delicate! [*Pause*] Don't you think so, Prince? Fritz?

FREDERICK
Yes, Majesty.

FREDERICK WILLIAM [*after a pause*]
Is that all? Isn't the artist to be congratulated?

FREDERICK
Congratulations, Majesty.

FREDERICK WILLIAM
But what do you think? Speak up!

[*No answer*]

Prince?

GENERAL

Majesty, in spite of the humor of the piece, *I* see decent bright colors, and solid brushwork. The costume is painted perfectly. Like the son, the father *does* have his artistic side!

[*Uneasy silence.* FREDERICK WILLIAM *glares at the* GENERAL.]

FREDERICK WILLIAM

Who asked you? Be careful. You can bite your hands tomorrow for what you say to the King today. Isn't that right, General?

GENERAL [*quickly*]

Yes, Majesty.

FREDERICK WILLIAM

Artists paint, play music, write poems, but in the affairs of men, they make fools of themselves! I never met one yet who said the proper thing. Did you, gentlemen?

CABINET

No, Majesty.

FREDERICK WILLIAM

Did you, Fritz? [*Pause*] *Did* you, Fritz?

FREDERICK [*softly*]

No, Majesty.

FREDERICK WILLIAM

But to be fair, it is capable work. Because the artist chose a subject he could understand! How do you think I got it to keep still? Hold that fine pose? By observation, that's how! Who is it? Come, gentlemen? Who is it?

CABINET

Why—why—

FREDERICK WILLIAM

It's him! It's a portrait of the Prince! That's you, Fritz! My gift! You'll hang it in your room and you'll look at it every day, and, by God, you can't say *now* there's no artistic activity in this court! Can you? Can you, Fritz?

FREDERICK

No, Majesty.

FREDERICK WILLIAM

God, he's stiff as a poker. Plays the flute, but can't take a joke. Writes verse, but can't talk honestly with a roomful of men. Prince, your philosophers and your artists are all fudge and pasty pudding. They make pretty sounds. They paint pretty pictures. They think they know everything. More than that is needed to preserve our nation! I'm doing my best to make you see that, Son.

FREDERICK

I thank you, Majesty.

FREDERICK WILLIAM

Majesty! Is that the only way you talk to me now?

FREDERICK

Forgive me, Papa.

FREDERICK WILLIAM

Here, maybe your fine attendants will learn something from this little school anyway. You, Fredersdorf, you're an honest man, you served well in the Army, I know that. Watch over this little egg. And you, Katte, well, you're too pretty for my taste, I'll be damned if you don't look like a girl, but you *can* ride a horse, I've seen you. You watch him too. Agreed?

Act I

GENERAL [*on his feet*]
  Nothing. Nothing at all, Majesty.

FREDERICK WILLIAM
  What did he say!

FREDERICK [*ashen*]
  I shall look where I please.

BISHOP
  The Prince is drunk, Sire, and not responsible for what he says.

DOCTOR
  A little tipsy, Sire, that's all. It was nothing.

[*The King lurches to his feet, spilling beer, dropping his pipe.*]

FREDERICK WILLIAM
  You fop, you goddamned little girl! Monkey, baboon!

[*He lunges toward* FREDERICK *who lunges toward him. Both are held back.*]

FREDERICK
  I will look where I please! But I *do* love you. I love you, Majesty!

BISHOP
  There, Sire. Did you hear that? Bravo, Prince.

[FREDERICK, *held by* FREDERSDORF *and* KATTE, *holds out both arms.*]

FREDERICK
  You believe any lie about me anyone tells you, so you can despise me. [*He points to the* POTSDAM GIANT.] For not being that. Because I'm not that thing! I don't hate you for it. [*Weeping*] I love you! Papa, you drunken fool! I love you!

GENERAL
> There, Majesty. Your son loves his father. A fine boy, a wonderful young man.

FREDERICK WILLIAM
> What's he saying now?

BISHOP
> The Prince just said that although the King has forced him to drink too much, he loves him deeply. Deeply.

FREDERICK WILLIAM
> Pretending. Always pretending.

CHANCELLOR
> On my word of honor, he is drunk, Sire.

FREDERICK WILLIAM
> He's sly, like a woman. Go to bed, Prince. Somebody put the fool to bed.

> [*He chokes and coughs violently.* FREDERICK *frees himself.*]

FREDERICK
> Your hand, Papa.

> [FREDERICK WILLIAM *slowly holds it out.* FREDERICK *walks to his father, takes his hand, kisses it, then suddenly falls on his knees, embracing the boots of the King.*]

> [*Sobbing*] Lies, lies, lies, lies! I love and adore you!

> [FREDERICK WILLIAM *puts both hands on* FREDERICK'*s shoulders.*]

FREDERICK WILLIAM
> All right. Good. Good! [*He looks around with bleary eyes.*] You see. He is a man of honor. You see? [FREDERICK WILLIAM *keeps patting his son on the back and shoulders, but these caresses become harder and stronger. Finally,*

Act I

they fall upon FREDERICK *as open blows.*] Listen to me, Fritz. Be open with your father. Straightforward, aboveboard. No foppishness, be a man. Keep your head clear, remember that! Don't let them cheat you. Always watch the Treasury, don't let them beggar you! Keep the Army strong! Guns and hard troops, soldiers who know how to fight. And a sound economy! Don't let them fool you! Strong, be strong! [*His fists are now clenched, the blows fall in a manic rhythm. Murderously, he beats his son.*] Strong! Strong! Strong! Strong!

[FREDERICK *reels away, battered, and falls to the floor.* FREDERSDORF *and* KATTE *help him to his feet and walk him out of the room.*]

Now everyone will say that I have treated my son badly. They will have a low opinion of me. Well, that's all right. That's all right. So do I.

[*Exeunt* FREDERICK WILLIAM *with his* POTSDAM GIANT *and his* CABINET. *Drums. The stage is cleared. Enter* FREDERICK, *wearing a scarlet cloak. With him is* FREDERSDORF.]

FREDERICK
Thanks. Now get away from here.

FREDERSDORF
You must take me with you. What am I without you?

FREDERICK
You won't be safe. That settles that. Hurry now. Goodbye.

FREDERSDORF
No. I will never desert you.

FREDERICK
It's an order, do you understand?

[FREDERSDORF *pulls the Prince to him roughly, then exits. Enter the* CHANCELLOR.]

CHANCELLOR

Good evening, Your Royal Highness. You are out rather late.

FREDERICK

What of that?

CHANCELLOR

Well, it is a bit unusual to find the Crown Prince strolling about alone at one end of the Kingdom, in the middle of the night.

FREDERICK

You mind your behavior. It's a nice evening, and I wish to enjoy it, alone.

CHANCELLOR

Not quite alone. A few hopes, I think, keep you company. You see a new world just over the French border. All your youth is coiled like a spring, to catapult you into it. A fresh world. A new universe. Escape.

FREDERICK

I don't care for your company. Leave me alone.

CHANCELLOR

I'm sorry, that's impossible. Your adventure was discovered several days ago. Lieutenant Hans Katte will not join you here tonight as you expected. He has been arrested, found guilty of desertion, and sentenced to life imprisonment.

FREDERICK

What are you talking about?

CHANCELLOR

Your letters were carelessly sent. As telltale as that scarlet cloak. They were easily intercepted, read, and passed on. There will be no more horses, no Hans Katte, and no daring night gallop over the French border. Your father

Act I

has known for days that you and Katte, desperate children, were deserting together.

[*Enter the* GENERAL.]

GENERAL
I regret to inform Your Royal Higness that you are from this moment under arrest. If you resist our orders from His Majesty, we must shoot to kill.

CHANCELLOR
Please respect us. We must do our duty.

FREDERICK
What will happen to me?

GENERAL
The question is in the hands of the King. Traitors must be punished.

[*Drums. Enter the* BISHOP.]

BISHOP
Compose yourself, Your Royal Highness. Everything that lives must die. It is the will of God. Submit yourself, and pray for your kingdom, for your father, and for your immortal soul.

[*As the* BISHOP *speaks, the* CHANCELLOR *takes off* FREDERICK's *cloak.*]

FREDERICK
But I am his son! I am the Prince! He won't kill me! He can't! He wouldn't dare!

BISHOP
He is the King. He can do what he likes, my son.

FREDERICK
No! No! I don't believe it.

[*The drums are heard steadily and with full force. Enter*

SOLDIER 1 *with a leather pouch in his hands. The* GENERAL *receives the letter inside, returns the pouch to* SOLDIER 1.]

GENERAL

Royal Highness, His Majesty the King decrees you will now hear his judgment.

[*Drums. Enter the* EXECUTIONER, *in black, carrying a chopping block. He sets it down and stands with his axe in his hands.*]

FREDERICK

It's not possible. Papa! Papa!

[*Drums. Enter* SOLDIERS 1 *and* 2. *Between them, enter* KATTE.]

GENERAL

The verdict of life imprisonment against Lieutenant Hans Katte has been personally countermanded by the King of Prussia. Lieutenant Hans Katte is sentenced to death by decapitation.

FREDERICK

Katte! Katte! In heaven's name, no! Oh Katte, for God's sake, forgive me! [*He embraces* KATTE.]

KATTE [*shaking*]

May you achieve all your dreams. I am happy to die for so fine a prince.

GENERAL

The execution will take place immediately, under the following conditions.

[*Drums.* KATTE *opens the collar of his shirt. He crosses himself, mutters "Lord Jesus," and then kneels, placing his neck upon the block.*]

Please respect me, Your Royal Highness. Your father decrees you must watch.

Act I

FREDERICK
Katte! Katte! Katte!

[*The drums stop. The* EXECUTIONER *raises his axe.*]

[*Screaming*] Katte!

Curtain

ACT II

The King

It is the present again. SOLDIER 1 *is onstage. Enter* SOLDIER 2.

SOLDIER 1
Well, where is it?

SOLDIER 2
Just what I was afraid of. They've already buried it.

SOLDIER 1
What?

SOLDIER 2
The King was at war. What else were they going to do?

SOLDIER 1
Then that takes care of that.

SOLDIER 2
You think so? He said he wanted to see the body.

SOLDIER 1
Now? Maybe the rain stopped him. Christ, he's seventy-three years old, after all.

SOLDIER 2
At his reviews last year I watched him ride in the rain for six hours. He'll come galloping over that hill before you know where you are. There's only one thing to do. Dig it up again.

SOLDIER 1
That's disgusting. I won't do it.

Act II

SOLDIER 2
> Then maybe you'd rather tell the King, who left a battlefield and rode all night in the rain, that nobody thought he was coming, so the body is already buried under six feet of dirt.

SOLDIER 1
> Where?

SOLDIER 2
> On the edge of the palace grounds, near the backroads. Come on.

SOLDIER 1
> God dammit, it's revolting. The thing isn't even human.

SOLDIER 2
> It's all we can do.

[*Exeunt* SOLDIERS 1 *and* 2. *The past again. Bells ring, deep and mournful. From opposite directions, enter the* CABINET, *each member thinking his own thoughts.*]

GENERAL
> Over, thank heaven. A battle plan, you know, is simplicity itself compared to a state funeral.

CHANCELLOR
> It was flawless, magnificent. Congratulations.

GENERAL
> Thank you, I thought the shrouded throne was a nice touch.

CHANCELLOR [*to the* GENERAL]
> I'm not exactly sure I should be the one to tell you this, but only an hour ago I received some instructions about the finances of the Royal Guards. His father's giants, I mean. But, of course, you knew about it some time ago.

GENERAL
   I beg your pardon?

CHANCELLOR
   Yes, I wondered if you'd been told.

GENERAL
   Told what, please?

CHANCELLOR
   They're junked. No more money for them. Dismissed. Today. The roads of Prussia at this moment hold several thousand bewildered giants, seven feet tall, wandering about, wondering what to do with themselves. It does seem you would have been informed.

GENERAL
   Deliberate, silly gesture. I won't be surprised if he commands every soldier to carry a flute instead of a rifle, and march past the reviewing stand on tiptoe. Playing French music. Skipping off to battle maneuvers under a dancing master.

CHANCELLOR
   Delightful notion. But is it so funny after all? He is the King, don't you understand? It is true, impossible as it may seem to all of us.

BISHOP
   What kind of king, then, do you make out of a French fop?

CHANCELLOR
   That will depend on us. On our skill.

GENERAL
   Exactly. Just how skillful are we these days?

CHANCELLOR
   Let's find out. Perhaps we might discuss further the health of the King—but frankly, you understand.

Act II

DOCTOR
> I understand. I am glad to see you concerned about it.

GENERAL
> Oh, please.

DOCTOR
> All right. He won't last a year.

CHANCELLOR
> Really?

DOCTOR
> Really. Our new King is the ruins of a twenty-nine-year nervous disaster. He is a hanging garden of uprooted nerves. For ten years he has slaved like a common clerk to please his father. Drills himself like a Hussar. Does everything he hates and despises. And of course, his marriage. Well, do you know that four years after the wedding that wretched woman still primps and waits for him every night? Pitiful.

GENERAL
> Pity them both. That little frump is quite enough to turn anyone's stomach. His father's final blow, marrying him to a housefrau.

BISHOP
> His religion, I'm sorry to say, is as bleak as his sex. God is the way everything works. That's all. And I will be very amused to see what happens to the Treasury when this philosophical hedonist gets his hands on it, as he will today.

CHANCELLOR
> Not very skillful, are we?

GENERAL
> No. Gentlemen, let us bury these bristling rivalries. Prussia has inherited God knows what for a king. We

must face our plain duty. The survival of this nation is our responsibility.

DOCTOR

That's very inspiring. However, we must learn to trust each other first. You'll admit, it's a slight obstacle.

CHANCELLOR

We know what he is. A frightened little fool who wallows in sensual pleasures to escape the burdens of his existence. We have only to agree among ourselves which way we pull him by the nose. Otherwise, along with being eaten alive by the rest of Europe, we'll die of boredom at concerts and poetry readings.

BISHOP

I deplore your harshness, but not your logic.

GENERAL

Army, Church, Government, Science. I think we are each of us familiar, to say the least, with the ambitions of the other. Well, do we fight among ourselves, or do we march together for the preservation of our land?

DOCTOR

We fight among ourselves. But sensibly. Which means we let each other know what we are telling the King.

BISHOP

Gross expression, but accurate logic. Now, how much do we tell the King?

CHANCELLOR

As little as possible.

ALL

Agreed!

[*Enter* FREDERSDORF. *He carries a gilded chair and puts it down.*]

Act II

FREDERSDORF
>The King.

[*Enter* FREDERICK. *He is now close to thirty, but looks older. Ten years have passed since* KATTE's *execution. Until this moment, he has subjugated himself completely to his father's will. He carries his flute.*]

FREDERICK
>Well, gentlemen, my congratulations on the funeral. He might have preferred something less elaborate, but he had no choice, did he? Now the people think they loved him all the time, and it was very moving. Tomorrow morning I want to see all the accounts of that spectacle, down to the last penny. That was a lot of velvet drapery you had hanging about. If anyone made a killing on it, I warn you, the accounts will not be passed. Now, who measured him?

DOCTOR
>I did, Majesty, as you commanded.

FREDERICK
>And?

DOCTOR
>At death, your father's body measured eight feet six inches around the stomach.

FREDERICK
>Really? That much?

DOCTOR
>I measured him myself, Sire.

FREDERICK
>I win, Fredersdorf! You were off by two feet! Gentlemen, with that we will pass over the domestic torments of this great Prince. He was an excellent administrator. He was an honest man who worked hard for his people. He

was my father, and I loved him. But now he is gone. Period of mourning, one month. At the conclusion of that time, a celebration here—a fête, if you please, *à la française*. I am composing a concerto for flute and orchestra for the occasion. I have drawn up certain recommendations and procedures for each of you to follow. I expect you to sweat just as much over your offices as I do over my music. Fredersdorf.

[FREDERSDORF *nods and leaves.* FREDERICK *plays a quick arpeggio on his flute.*]

In the meantime, I invite each of you in turn to dine with me, alone. Great men, such as yourselves, must be considered singly. One at a time, as you deserve. All together, you tend to distract one another, like children.

[FREDERICK *plays a quick scale on his flute as* FREDERSDORF *comes in with a stack of papers. The* CABINET *buzzes among itself.* FREDERICK *plays a delicate trill, lingering on the last note until they are quiet.*]

So here we are. With Europe at the keyhole. You see, my father left me, if I may be permitted the expression, a kind of hermaphrodite. Not quite a kingdom, but a little bit more than an electorate. Now, at such a dramatic moment, with all the world waiting to see just what sexual organs we choose to expose, can we afford to disappoint? I am delighted to see that each of you looks so eager for the tasks that lie ahead of you. As for me, well, this afternoon I must write to the King of France, compose a largo, make up a poem for Voltaire, and alter the constitution of the Army. Fredersdorf has your instructions. Good morning.

[*Music:* FREDERICK's *C-Major Concerto for Flute and Orchestra, First Movement.* FREDERICK *settles onto his*

Act II   51

throne, or stands upstage and plays his flute, while the CABINET *delivers proclamations.*]

DOCTOR

His Majesty announces the European publication of his book, the *Anti-Machiavel*. This work, edited by Monsieur Voltaire of France, is the open refutation of the doctrines of Machiavelli, who would rule by deceit.

GENERAL

His Majesty announces the abolition of physical torture. His Majesty requires his own review of all sentences of death and imprisonment. His Majesty informs his courts that judges will serve, not punish, the people.

CHANCELLOR

Taxes are reduced, embargoes lifted, relief projects ordained, school systems commanded, hunting privileges of the nobility abolished. Petitioners may come to the King at any time. They will be heard.

BISHOP

Every man in Prussia is at liberty to find his own way up to heaven. Go to church, any kind of church you please, or stay at home and sleep, as you wish. [*Under his breath*] Oh, my God.

[*Music swells.*]

The King declares complete freedom of the Prussian newspapers. A newspaper must be free, you know, simply to be interesting.

CHANCELLOR

There is a new Academy of Science! A new Academy of Art! A new opera house! A Royal Gazette, in French! The King will be a frequent contributor! So will we!

GENERAL

The King orders the creation of sixteen new battalions

within the month. A new manual of Prussian drill will be issued tomorrow. Military arrogance will be severely punished. Any officer responsible for disrespect toward private citizens will be court-martialed within the hour.

DOCTOR

To the masters of darkness, superstition, and oppression, the King offers swift destruction if they approach his Kingdom. But to all enlightened spirits of modern Europe, in this Age of Reason, Frederick II, King of Prussia, offers his welcome, his protection, and the liberty to work with him for the advancement of humanity. Long may he reign!

[*Exit the* CABINET. *Enter a small skeletal man with a cane. He is very ugly and very elegant. His carbuncle eyes glitter.* FREDERICK *takes him by the arm fondly. They stroll together about the stage.*]

VOLTAIRE

A young prince once wrote to an ancient scribbler and sent him an "Ode Against Flattery." This doubtful old man of letters thought then that a prince writing odes against flattery was as unlikely as a pope composing hymns against the Church. However, they became friends. They published a book together, condemning Machiavelli. But the cynical old historian reflected that the first thing true pupils of Machiavelli do is write books against him. Still, he could not help being filled with hope. Was it possible that here could be the philosopher-prince of whom poor Plato dreamed, and here a weathered poet to guide him? Miracle of miracles, the Prince survives, to become the King who will defend Europe against tyranny and superstition. With all my heart, I salute our Solomon of the North.

FREDERICK

Perhaps Don Quixote rather than Solomon, but we will

Act II

see. At any rate, it was to you the Prince said all his prayers. [*Suddenly kneeling*] He knelt by his bed and prayed to his saint: the greatest writer in the world, and the only fearless man in Europe, Voltaire. And now, my Deity, are you pleased with the apprentice who has loved you?

VOLTAIRE [*raising him gently*]
I will sing his praise until the day I die! Most kings are frightened to hear the truth, yet you undertake to teach it.

FREDERICK
No, no, it is you who must teach! You must keep faith with the Prince by instructing the King, as always.

VOLTAIRE
Then let me wonder if the poet, the musician, can so easily exist within the King. The truth is, great artists, like great kings, sometimes conceive great contempt for shivering mankind.

FREDERICK
I have suffered so much from that disease in others, I do not think it will infect me now.

VOLTAIRE
I will be corrected when I know you have not succumbed to that final plague of kings, and artists.

FREDERICK
Well, the greatest of writers sometimes contract that little malady themselves.

VOLTAIRE
The only difference between the private passions of kings and writers is that the latter are ridiculous. Rule your Prussian Kingdom, Your Majesty. Voltaire, with all of Europe, stands amazed at your brilliance.

FREDERICK [*after a pause*]

When are you coming to live with me? These brief visits are almost worse than none. You will stand officially among my titles: Frederick, King of Prussia, Prince Elector of Brandenburg, and Possessor of Voltaire! I will give you the greatest royal welcome any citizen has ever received.

VOLTAIRE

That would make an old man very happy. But other friendships hold me at home and will not let me leave. To me you were always more a man than a prince, and you will, without doubt, permit me, my Lord, to prefer my friends even to kings. [*Exit* VOLTAIRE.]

FREDERICK

All in good time, all in good time.

[*Enter the* CABINET.]

CHANCELLOR

Majesty, we hasten to inform you of the death of the Austrian Emperor.

DOCTOR

The Holy Roman Empire of the German Nation must now be led by his only heir, the twenty-three-year-old daughter. It is a ticklish moment, Sire.

BISHOP

Peace in Europe depends upon swift support of Maria Theresa's rightful claim to her throne. Your Majesty is aware that every shark in the water waits to see her claim challenged. What is worse, the lady is in delicate health—quite pregnant, alas—and cannot endure a coronation for some time.

GENERAL

To support Your Majesty's recent declarations of loyalty

Act II

to the Empire, I propose maneuvers to strengthen both borderlands.

BISHOP
I propose divine services imploring God to bless this union of Austria and Prussia.

CHANCELLOR
I propose further endorsement of all Your Majesty's treaties with Austria to publicly demonstrate your loyalty to your sworn word.

DOCTOR
And I propose a mutual congress of artistic and scientific intercourse. Its theme: Peace!

CHANCELLOR
Shall we place these suggestions into concrete form, Sire? It would be well to make yourself heard at once. The world awaits the first firm action of the philosopher-King.

[*They all stare at him, waiting. He is staring blankly into space, tapping his flute against his boot.*]

DOCTOR
Shall we continue, Majesty?

FREDERICK
No. [*He points suddenly to a handsome young lieutenant, who has been standing in the background.*] Who is that young officer there?

GENERAL
My aide, Sire. Lieutenant Kort.

FREDERICK
What name?

KORT
Kort, Majesty.

FREDERICK

Well then. What do you think about it?

KORT

Majesty, I cannot say. I am a very young and inexperienced officer.

FREDERICK

Quite right. A child, in fact. What happens to children, Lieutenant?

KORT

They change, Sire. They grow.

FREDERICK

Larger, in fact. And how does the child feel then?

KORT

Better, bigger. Resolved.

FREDERICK

Perfect. What then?

KORT

He must continue to grow. The child must improve himself. Do more.

FREDERICK

The first law of life: Impressions received in childhood cannot be erased from the soul. As this handsome baby so clearly sees. Gentlemen, that means growth. Enlargement, if you will. I hope you have not forgotten my father's claim to twenty thousand square miles of Austria? To all of the Silesian province?

CHANCELLOR

Majesty, that disputed claim lies buried in the past. You cannot possibly hope to resurrect it now.

FREDERICK

And who will tell me not to? Control yourself when you

Act II

advise the King. You may bite your tongue tomorrow for what you say today.

GENERAL

Sire, consider military reality. You will have to fight. Your father did create an impressive force on the parade ground, but he was always careful never to take it into the field of battle.

FREDERICK

Because my father's soldiers are handsome, you think them only pretty. General, I'm going to show you that a Prussian soldier fights even better than he looks. This month, gentlemen, it is not going to be a question of philosophy, poetry, and music, but of gunpowder, trenches, and steel. Arrange yourselves accordingly.

BISHOP

Attack Austria? To invade her now? Such careless levity, Sire, is absolutely unheard of!

FREDERICK

Well, I'm trying to be original.

DOCTOR

Can His Majesty be fully aware of the consequences of his proposals?

FREDERICK

I am aware of my duty, sir, and the life to which I was born. This little project will bring a reputation to the King and power to the State, both very necessary before peace and music can be maintained. In two days we cross the Silesian border, into a defenseless province, against a pregnant woman, and I suggest you all be at my side, singing loudly. Lieutenant!

KORT

Majesty!

FREDERICK

To me!

[*Drums. The lieutenant helps* FREDERICK *into a military coat, hands him a sword, and takes his flute. All exeunt. Enter* VOLTAIRE. *Light on him upstage.*]

VOLTAIRE

Majesty?

[*Enter* FREDERICK.]

FREDERICK

Oh, you reform the spirit of the age, and leave the geography to me. From this fat rump of Austria, let me carve away one tiny piece for myself.

VOLTAIRE

And go to war? Why suffer that? Why suffer at all? [*Pause*] Why don't you conquer Naples? You could give flute concerts under the southern stars. I would visit you and be your agreeable courtier. But Silesia? A rocky northern province of Austria, known for its cheese?

FREDERICK

I am about to destroy a city or be destroyed myself. You make jokes. But if I attacked the Vatican tomorrow, instead of Kesseldorf, and hung the Pope by his heels, you would rejoice, write an "Ode to Freedom," and call me a hero. If God really wanted the world bathed in blood, he'd have it ruled by writers.

VOLTAIRE

God, in whom neither of us believes, leaves these matters, Majesty, to us.

FREDERICK

Us?

[*Drums. Music. Exit* VOLTAIRE. *Enter the* CABINET.]

Act II

BISHOP

With the blessings of Almighty God, the King seeks justice in a righteous war. In the name of the Father, and of the Son, and of the Holy Ghost.

DOCTOR

Men of Prussia! The King has noticed that we are now surrounded by ladies. Elizabeth in Russia. Maria Theresa in Austria, and Pompadour in the bedroom of the King of France. Follow him now and impress upon them a new birth of Prussian manhood.

GENERAL

The King of Prussia offers the Queen of Austria the protection of his allies and of his Army. In return, he asks for the province of Silesia, and he will accept nothing less. If it is not offered to him with good grace, he will take it.

CHANCELLOR

Courage! We have a great King, a good Army, and money in the Treasury. Our cause is just, and our resources prepared.

FREDERICK

And besides all that, I want to see my name in the newspapers!

[*Drums. Music*]

Prussians! Our fate now lies in the hands of Fortune! All that remains is to fight bravely and do what we can to alter Chance! Farewell! I follow you to the rendezvous of Fame, which now awaits us all!

[*Exeunt* FREDERICK *and the* CABINET. *Cannonfire.* FREDERICK *invades Silesia. Enter* FREDERICK, *alone, his flute in one hand, his sword in the other. He looks up at the sky.*]

FREDERICK

Oh, my great poor fat fool of a father. Today as I rode to battle, I passed a farmhouse. A woman was standing under an apple tree, scolding her little boy who had climbed up to the topmost branch and would not come down. I stopped to see what was the matter. The boy was three years old. His father was dead, and he had climbed the tree when he was told his father went to heaven, to be just that much closer to him. Am I any different, the King, riding to war? What are you doing up there? Who gets your blows on his back? Do you throw inkpots at the white angels? Do you curse when they try to sing? Is your belly still eight feet six inches fat? [*Tears roll down his cheeks. Cannons roar in the distance. He holds up the sword and the flute.*] What do you think of your little fop who plays the flute? Would *you* take the field against him? And if you could really be in heaven, and I should one day stand before you again, would you promise to be what you were, and if I conquer the world, strike me just as hard?

[*Exit* FREDERICK. *Enter the* GENERAL *and* KORT.]

GENERAL

God dammit! Why didn't he let me attack? We had them in Mollwitz drinking beer and singing songs. God dammit! Now they know where we are! Madman! Lunatic!

KORT

The King!

[*Enter* FREDERICK.]

FREDERICK

You may attack now, if you please.

GENERAL

Why not three hours ago? Three hours ago, Majesty!

Act II

FREDERICK

I reserve command of this little venture to myself alone. The world shall not think the King of Prussia marches to war under a tutor. If you can gain sufficient control of yourself, we will proceed.

GENERAL

Majesty, in the name of God, put up your sword and let me lead the Army. You will be killed and everything ended.

FREDERICK

That's stupid. Of course I must lead the Army. Get hold of yourself. You look scared to death. [*To* KORT] And you, you pretty little thing, get on your horse and fight for your country! General?

[*Explosions. Rifle fire.* FREDERICK, *the* GENERAL, *and* KORT *exeunt and re-enter.*]

FREDERICK

What happened? What happened?

GENERAL

It's over. That's what happened. The Austrian cavalry crushed our center. It's hopeless!

FREDERICK

Do you mean to tell me I've lost?

GENERAL

All over, Sire. Full retreat or we will be massacred! Lieutenant! The King's horse!

FREDERICK

Well, Jesus Christ.

KORT

This way! This way, Majesty!

[*Exeunt* FREDERICK *and* KORT.]

GENERAL

Now, God dammit, maybe I can get something done! Major! Regroup artillery! Colonel, the infantry out of the woods! Cavalry and assault on left flanks!

[*Exit the* GENERAL. *Sounds of war. Enter the* GENERAL *and* KORT.]

GENERAL

Where is he?

KORT

In that farmhouse. In the barn. He tried to get into the garrison last night but some fool shot at him. He's been holed up in there all night long, thinking he lost the battle, crying and writing verses.

GENERAL

We would have lost it if I hadn't got rid of him. Does he know I countered and won?

[*Enter* FREDERICK.]

FREDERICK

He does. Congratulations. You are promoted. Decorated. Savior of Prussia, you have rescued the Army and the King. Now listen. Either I win these battles, or we all go down to hell together. That's how that works! For my part, General, I will stay in school. I will learn your strategy and you will learn to obey my orders. Now get me back on that battlefield!

[*Cannonfire. Red light. Explosion.* KORT *falls to his knees and cries out in agony.* FREDERICK *turns around and runs to him. He falls on his body.*]

Die quietly, can't you?

[*He rises.* SOLDIERS 1 *and* 2 *take away the body of the*

Act II

lieutenant. Enter VOLTAIRE. *He stands by* FREDERICK *and listens.*]

We go to war, and spill our blood. So much for the national glory. From how many points of view, philosopher, may the same object be seen?

VOLTAIRE

Philosopher, from what point of view do you choose to look?

FREDERICK

My own. Every ruler is obliged to misuse his power, in his own way.

VOLTAIRE

But, my author of the *Anti-Machiavel*, must he do so with such obvious relish?

FREDERICK

Yes. Otherwise, he could not do it at all. Any man who rules a nation, becomes, in time, a maniac. The only victory over that is to be aware of it.

VOLTAIRE

Are you, my Lord, aware of it?

FREDERICK

I think so. My military strategy is, I admit, a bit radical. I will not pretend I always know what possesses me. But I do know what I am after. I will win this war. Because I alone know how desperate everything is, that every moment is a matter of life and death. I am scrupulous. I was well schooled in lunacy, and in all the household origins of global treachery.

VOLTAIRE

I cannot match a poet who also leads an Army, or a king whose music is as dazzling as his sword. No man can speak with all the astounding authority you alone possess.

FREDERICK

This war will not last forever. When it's over, I will break my sword. I will go home and be tame. I won't so much as attack a cat.

VOLTAIRE

Then you will be Frederick the Great, and all your battles truly won. Achieve that victory, on that battlefield, and Voltaire will die at the feet of such a hero.

FREDERICK [*after a pause*]

When are you coming to live with me? You will have to sooner or later. My court is the only place that can tolerate you. I will possess you, great man. Wait and see.

VOLTAIRE

I look forward to that day when my obligations will permit it. I have the honor at this moment, to remain Your Majesty's devoted servant, in France.

FREDERICK

Devoted if I win, a servant hardly. No more visits. No more visits.

[*Exit* VOLTAIRE. *Enter* FREDERSDORF.]

FREDERSDORF

All those spices for dinner, and then playing right afterward. Your color is bad—liverish. How are your hemorrhoids?

FREDERICK

All right. How are yours?

FREDERSDORF

Terrible.

Act II

FREDERICK
> Fine. We will suffer together.

FREDERSDORF
> Majesty.

FREDERICK
> Yes?

FREDERSDORF
> Majesty, the Queen is here.

FREDERICK
> I beg your pardon?

FREDERSDORF
> The Queen is here. In camp. She says she must see you.

FREDERICK
> Why, my old cow. Christ in heaven, Solomon had a thousand wives and they weren't enough. I have one, and that's one too many. All right, bring her here. Get her something to sit on, and some brandy and coffee for me.

> [*Enter* THE QUEEN.]

> Well?

> [*In her heavy traveling clothes,* THE QUEEN *stands trembling before him. She is a very awkward, very plain woman. She has never in her life opposed anyone.*]

THE QUEEN
> I have been told that your losses have been terrible. That you are in great danger of losing the war. I thought you might let me see you, and I determined I would come and ask you for this audience. I am your wife. This is the only time I have asked it of you, after all.

FREDERICK
> Now, that's the truth. You have always been the most faithful creature in the universe, and I owe you the respect you demand. But I must confess, I am astonished at you for getting up the gumption to demand it, and I have fought four battles in two months and I'm tired. You really must be quick.

THE QUEEN
> I will try.

> [FREDERSDORF *brings in a table with brandy and coffee, then moves to the shadows and waits.* FREDERICK *pours coffee, and listens.*]

THE QUEEN [*stammering*]
> Is . . . is . . . my husband well?

FREDERICK
> Oh madam, please.

THE QUEEN
> I beg your pardon. I can't . . . you . . . this isn't easy for me.

FREDERICK
> I knew you'd begin that way, God bless you. You are being very brave, just like a soldier. I know what it means for you to come to see me. Compose yourself, and say what you came to say. Coffee?

THE QUEEN
> No, thank you. But I will take some brandy, if I may.

FREDERICK [*amazed*]
> My dear woman, the next thing I know you will grab my sword and rush off to fight my enemies. What has come over you?

Act II

THE QUEEN

Oh, no, nothing has come over me. There have been no miraculous transformations. I am still the ignorant and ugly girl your father picked for you from a sheepish crowd of dowdy virgins. But since our marriage, I have pleased myself to work as hard as I could, with these clumsy hands and these slow wits, to be your Queen . . .

FREDERICK

That's well said. You've composed your speech thoroughly. Drink a little brandy and continue. I'll wait.

THE QUEEN

I always knew I could never be a queen—or worthy of you. Your . . . neglect . . . and you must admit it has been breathtaking in its . . . completeness . . . like your other activities . . . well, I have taken it as another shameful matter of course, in this life of mine. I watch your greatness with agony and patience, and my pitiful lessons in embroidery and French have never stopped, not in seven years. That is a long time to study embroidery and French. Now I am getting older and uglier, if that is possible. I have given up my hope for children. Not heirs, simply children. I suppose I might have had those by a coachman, perhaps you wouldn't have minded at all. But no, I am still the same miserable girl, on my knees each night, praying to our heavenly Father for the love and safety of my husband. Surely I have aroused your disgust by now. [*She smiles, and drinks.*] But now, I find that I am beginning to laugh, as you do, when I think of certain things. My loutish ignorance, you see, is being simply worn away, not corrected by study or experience at all, but by sheer time and age, and all my frantic girlish fears go with it. Yesterday, when I heard you were almost killed, I could not keep from laughing. I remembered the first day we met, when I was dragged up before you by your father. Do you?

FREDERICK
Do I what, madam?

THE QUEEN
Remember that day?

FREDERICK
Well, I do now, thanks to this visit.

THE QUEEN
My father told me what to say, but he was as frightened as I was, poor man. And so I thought I would be myself, and trust to your understanding, and I stammered out to you my love of the Church and my devotion to God. And in a minute, you clearly said, not five feet away from me, to someone, "Jesus Christ, I would rather marry the biggest whore in Berlin than a pious woman." [*She drinks, and smiles.*] That has become, in the barbaric fullness of time, dear to me.

FREDERICK
Please. I cannot help the trick fate has played on me.

THE QUEEN
Ah, what trick is that? Is that why, timid and oafish spinster that I am, I find myself among soldiers and guns and war in the middle of the night, as in a melodrama for children? Perhaps I am not a woman at all, only a boy in disguise. Shall I now throw off these clothes and arouse something else beside seven years of the King's disgust? Would that be dramatic enough?

FREDERICK
Please, do not disgrace yourself.

THE QUEEN
No. I never have. I never will. But I can come to you, within all proper bounds, as I do tonight with the Austrian guns at your head, and ask for my place. I wish

Act II

to leave my castle that you so graciously built for me at the other end of Prussia, and accept with you whatever defeat you face. That is queenly, you must admit.

FREDERICK

I do admit it. But it is not possible.

THE QUEEN

Why, in the name of heaven? Do you think I will mind, now, a husband who hates women? Do you think, while your Kingdom crumbles around you, that I will scream at you because you have pretty page boys and handsome lieutenants in for breakfast? You have no qualms about the acrid scandal of your behavior, you even encourage it. Do you think I will give you a sermon on the matter? I implore you, let me go back to the place where we should live, and be no longer the same ridiculous figure as a Queen that I always was as a girl! Give me at least the protection of those walls, if nothing else! Is that outrageous?

FREDERICK [coldly]

Yes. Is there anything else?

THE QUEEN

There is. And you will hear it now, from my own mouth. I am a wife remarkable for her loutish stupidity, as you have said yourself, while treating me with perfect civility. I will not be civil now; I will be direct. Your table talk may be scandalous, but your bedroom, so I am told, is monastic. I do not believe your masquerades with page boys and soldiers. They did not ring true to me seven years ago; they don't now. So I ask you, if you must banish me back into the convent you have made of my life, to satisfy at least my female curiosity. And to forgive your wife one outburst of temper in seven barren years.

FREDERICK
Are you all right?

THE QUEEN
Oh, please. Please.

FREDERICK
Fredersdorf.

[FREDERSDORF *comes forward.*]

The Doctor, if you please. At once.

[FREDERSDORF *goes.* THE QUEEN *lifts her head. She is miserably ugly now, crying, and she is a little drunk.*]

I have always respected you for the brave acceptance of a miserable fate, being married to me. I respect you no less now for demanding a reason for that fate. You shall have it.

[*Enter the* DOCTOR.]

The Queen of Prussia, Doctor, wishes to know why it is that her husband, the King, has never consummated their union. Tell her.

DOCTOR [*under his breath*]
My God!

FREDERICK
Your embarrassment is altogether understandable. Take a minute to compose yourself. Then tell her the truth. She is waiting. [*He begins to play very softly on the flute.*]

DOCTOR
The King, as a young man, accompanied his father to the court of Poland. It was a licentious and immoral spectacle. His father's restraint was excessive. But the young Prince, given at last the occasion, indulged himself in

Act II   71

an excusable abundance of sexual pleasure. The King of Poland himself supplied the women. There were a great many of them.

FREDERICK

Go ahead.

DOCTOR

One was diseased. When the Prince returned to Prussia, he discovered that he was infected with a *gonorrhea maligna*. Caught in a boy's panic, ravaged by fears of his father discovering this hideous disgrace, the young Prince, in torment, submitted to the treatment of a doctor from Malchow, a quack. The treatment seemed successful. A few months passed. Then, doubled, the banked fires of the infection broke out again. In further panic, and now in real danger of gangrene, the Prince abandoned himself to more heroic treatment. He was operated upon. Badly. The infection was arrested, the disease continued its course. Not long afterward, you were married to him.

FREDERICK

You see, everything has a reason. You are quite right about my page boys. And my poems, and my table talk. It is a masquerade. But Europe must believe that the King of Prussia goes to bed with someone. Conclude, Doctor.

DOCTOR

Since his operation, His Majesty has not been able to bring himself to attempt the sexual act.

FREDERICK

Thank you.

[*Exit the* DOCTOR.]

Are you speechless now, all over again?

[THE QUEEN *stares at him. She puts her hands to her head, and she laughs.*]

I am delighted my sexual agony amuses you. And I admire your persistence, after seven years.

THE QUEEN

I will go home. I won't bother you again. And I will pray to God that I never, never cause anyone to lose any happiness as long as I live.

FREDERICK

That is both noble and generous. I regret I have already lost ours. Good night.

[*Exit* THE QUEEN. *The* DOCTOR *returns and stands watching* FREDERICK.]

Yes?

DOCTOR

Is it true?

FREDERICK

Pardon?

DOCTOR

Is it the truth? I have never examined you, after all. As far as I know, no one has. You have told me what happened to you. If I outlive you, I will publish it. I suppose it is what you have decided to make known about yourself, in years to come. But is it the truth?

FREDERICK

Everyone is full of courage tonight. It must be an epidemic. My poor old cow races through battlefields, and now you want to look at the balls of the King of Prussia. [*He smiles at the* DOCTOR.] God help you if you let that little publication go before I'm dead. If you outlive me,

Act II

that's another matter. Write your book then, and put what you please in it. Good night.

[*Exit the* DOCTOR. FREDERICK *sighs, looks at his flute. In a moment, enter the* CABINET.]

Yes, yes, breathing fire, everyone?

CHANCELLOR
The treasury is exhausted, Sire. There is no more money.

FREDERICK
Melt the silver plate. Refine it for bullets.

BISHOP
The people pray for you no longer. You are the Devil now, the anti-Christ.

GENERAL
The Army is very uneasy. Soldiers desert now by the battalion.

DOCTOR
Your health is shattered and you know it. You don't eat and you don't sleep. You will collapse in a month.

FREDERICK
But what, gentlemen, am I to do? Wash my face and hands and be marched upstairs to bed like a good child? We fight today! Christ or anti-Christ, I don't believe in either one. I will be buried under the ruins of every building in Austria before I yield to anyone. As for the soldiers who desert, I will shoot them myself, by the battalion, if I have to. March! Damn you, gentlemen, right now. March!

[*Exeunt the* CHANCELLOR, BISHOP, *and* DOCTOR. FREDERICK *and the* GENERAL *face one direction, ready for the Austrian attack. It does not come.*]

Why don't they attack?

GENERAL
 I don't know.

FREDERICK [*after a pause*]
 I do. They are afraid. Of me. They won't attack. I knew what I was doing, after all. It's over. Send the dispatches.

[*Exit the* GENERAL.]

And now we have a bigger kingdom to manage! We will manage it. We will work harder in peace than ever we fought in war. But today, like frivolous mortals, let us enjoy the fruits of victory!

[*Enter* FREDERSDORF, *slowly*.]

Fredersdorf. My God, what's wrong with you?

FREDERSDORF
 Why, I have given out, that's all. Did you think I would be about forever, to take care of you?

FREDERICK
 Don't speak that way to me! Doctor, the doctor!

FREDERSDORF
 When a man can't breathe, when he is as old and sick as I am, then he can't lift his head, and he dies. That's all there is to it, it seems.

FREDERICK [*embracing him*]
 I won't hear that! Bear up, for God's sake. It's an order, old man.

FREDERSDORF
 Now, now. Don't make my last act my only disobedience. I don't want to leave you. [*Exit* FREDERSDORF.]

FREDERICK
 Never mind. I am used to it. And Fortune may send me another friend. [*He bows his head.*] Now. I need you

Act II

now. Come to me. Come! [*He raises his head.*] Let my victory celebrations proceed!

[*Music. Enter* VOLTAIRE. FREDERICK *rushes to him. The light changes to a cold blue. Embracing,* FREDERICK *and* VOLTAIRE *stand motionless. It is the present again. There are dim lights downstage, where* SOLDIERS 1 *and* 2 *crouch. One has a shovel. They peer about on the darkened stage.*]

SOLDIER 1
Are you sure you know which one it is?

SOLDIER 2
Yes, yes, there, fourth from the left. See, the dirt is fresh. Hurry.

SOLDIER 1
What if we dig up the wrong one?

SOLDIER 2
Then God help us.

SOLDIER 1
Oh, it's awful. The thing is an animal, a bloody rotten animal.

SOLDIER 2
Well, ready?

SOLDIER 1
Ready.

[*Exeunt* SOLDIERS 1 *and* 2.]

Curtain

ACT III

The Philosopher

Flute music. The past again. The scene is Sans Souci, FREDERICK's *famous retreat.* FREDERICK, *the* CABINET, *and* VOLTAIRE *stand near elegant chairs around a table holding several decanters of different wines.* FREDERICK *offers a toast.*

FREDERICK

To the Holy Roman Empire, gentlemen. An ancient institution, a bit senile, even, and to the part Prussia must play in its future. To Change, which is inevitable, and to Chance, which, when boldly seized, may be a chief instrument in that Change. And, oh, yes! Gallantry insists! To the three empresses of Europe: Maria Theresa, Elizabeth, and Pompadour—their babies, their lovers, their venereal diseases—and their shocking female lust for the body of my nation! The Empire!

CABINET

The Empire!

VOLTAIRE

That is a remarkable toast, Your Majesty. To what sort of dinner, I wonder, is it a prelude? Gunpowder soup? Boot-leather pie?

FREDERICK

At dinner, the guest must trust his host. Your health!

[*They all sit.*]

Gentlemen, I am the luckiest of poets. I have my verses criticized by Voltaire himself. "Pooh, this is worthless. Wipe this out, for the love of God. This might pass. This

Act III

is tolerable." Once I remember: "Here you must be bold, Sire. Heroic! Strike!" [*Laughs*] But when I think about Europe, as I must, in exactly the same way he tells me to think about verses, he shudders and turns blue, with envy, perhaps, as well as alarm.

VOLTAIRE

Verses, Sire, even bad ones, are always heroic when their cause is enlightenment. Battles never are. They may be awesome, like cannibals, but never heroic.

FREDERICK

Oh, my fierce friend, I have often tried to imagine you with a sword instead of a pen, but it is hopeless. There is nothing more comical, gentlemen, than Voltaire before the facts of illness, war, taxes, and death. Our great advocate of human rights, the deadly enemy of religious superstition, becomes a jellyfish. Panic seizes him. I tell you, when he dies, he'll call in the parish priest.

VOLTAIRE

Who can say?

BISHOP

Has His Majesty succeeded in proving Voltaire pious after all? Not in the spirit or the intellect, but in the ordinary, perishable flesh?

FREDERICK

Have I?

VOLTAIRE

Not for a moment. [*To the* BISHOP] I am sorry to disappoint you, but no, I am not really pious. Unlike the Egyptians, I cannot worship crocodiles and onions. Unlike the young Jew who thought himself Dionysus reborn, I cannot worship myself upon the cross. I am always amazed by men who have the bad taste to speak for God.

BISHOP

That is because you want to do so yourself.

FREDERICK [*laughing*]

Bravo!

BISHOP

Voltaire amuses us. While we are laughing, he runs outside and nails up the doors of the Church.

VOLTAIRE

Not at all. Let us worship, by all means. Two or three times a year, in a beautiful temple with music, and thank God for life. There is one sun in the heavens. There is—perhaps—one God in the universe. Let us have one religion on earth. Then—perhaps—we may approach true brotherhood, forgive each other our private monstrosities, and heavens! is it possible? in that way fulfill the beautiful dreams of the Dionysian Jew.

FREDERICK

Horse shit. I will desert the Enlightened, and join the Bishop. [*To* VOLTAIRE] With your reputation for wit, it is indecent to solemnly tell us, "All men are brothers." Is that, finally, all that comes out of Voltaire's kitchen? If you blame me for cooking up the flesh of the enemies of Prussia, is that worse than serving your bland soup, fizzing with unphilosophical bromides like brotherly love? Men eat flesh. I didn't sign that into law. It's the way things are. So we eat flesh. But sip brotherly love, as some poets pretend we should, and help! nausea soon follows!

VOLTAIRE

But if we devour each other, Sire, who will be left to drink wine, make jokes, and spin out whimsical images? I have never understood why monarchs become so in-

Act III

fatuated with brotherly hatred, so bored by brotherly love.

FREDERICK

You know very well, we vomit brotherly love onto the council tables, and then go to the battlefield to be cleansed of the mess. Gentlemen, search below the sparkling words of the famous poet, and what do you always find lurking underneath? The palpitating perpetual motion that drives all his brilliance? Why, love. That is really all you preach. You are as wanton in philosophy as a whore in a dirty bed. Love each other. Every poet babbles about it, down there in the mines below the surface. Poetic love is the last word of the fop, the final reproach of the lunatic, the high priest of the suicide, and the first commandment of the insane.

VOLTAIRE

Sire—

FREDERICK

No, no! The body is honest, if the mind is not. It vomits!

VOLTAIRE

I confess, I cannot with reason set upon mankind the commandments of love. Men cannot love each other. It is not yet in their nature to do so. I cannot say, "Love each other," without being absurd. But I do say, I must say, what they *can* do. Stop killing each other!

FREDERICK

It is the same thing, my dear friend. One is just as impossible as the other. Man will never give up his right to violence. It is as necessary to him as his lust. Is that my fault? What would you have me do, your philosopher-King? I mean, actually *do?* Right now!

VOLTAIRE

Give back Silesia.

FREDERICK [shocked]
What?

VOLTAIRE
Give back the country you have conquered, and repair the alliance you have broken.

FREDERICK
Monsieur Voltaire, splendid critic, accept one elementary lesson from me. I keep a strong Army. So does everyone else with any sense. I hoard money. So does everyone else with any sense. And I piss on alliances! So does everyone else with any sense! "Stop killing each other!" Of course! All you need is the consent of Europe, and a few minor things like that. Alliances, peace treaties? They are marriage contracts! I promise to support this or that nation, just as the brave new husband promises to support his wife and satisfy all her lusts. But as in marriage, where that burning little cunt can soak up the husband's strength, so in continental negotiations can the bottomless demands of allies make faithfulness intolerable! Then *nothing* can keep the man from getting a divorce! Have I reassured you, my dear friend?

VOLTAIRE
You replace all my doubts. With others.

FREDERICK [after a pause]
Four wines? Four wines? What are four wines doing here? Who's responsible? It's diabolical! Two wines! Only *two* wines before dinner! I drew up that order myself! Where is that cock-sucking steward! Waste! Ridiculous! Waste! Waste! [He storms out.]

VOLTAIRE [after a pause]
I will write a dictionary, for men in power. "My friend" means "my slave." "My dear friend" means "I hate you."

Act III

"Have dinner with me" means "I will tear the skin off you tonight to pass the evening."

[*There is an awkward silence. Then* FREDERICK *enters carrying a painting we have seen before, its cover tattered now.*]

FREDERICK
Well, well, forgive my outburst. Those scoundrels in the kitchens will beggar me yet. [*He beams at* VOLTAIRE.] But now, gentlemen, a pleasure. A feast for the eye. Yesterday, I discovered a portrait of Voltaire! Painted long ago, by a seer, a visionary, who foresaw the glory of the future. [*To* VOLTAIRE] Are you ready for this revelation? The likeness may overwhelm you.

VOLTAIRE
I am quite ready, Your Majesty, for anything.

FREDERICK
Splendid. Portrait of the great Voltaire! *Voilà!*

[*He displays the old painting of the monkey.* FREDERICK *roars with laughter. The* CABINET *joins him.*]

Perfection! It's you, dear friend! Down to the last detail! Well, what do you think of it?

VOLTAIRE
It is a bad painting of a monkey. What did you expect?

FREDERICK
You don't see the likeness? [*To the* CABINET] He doesn't see the likeness. Perhaps that is because, in this world, monkeys receive so much praise that it turns their heads. There are women, for instance, who adore this one. Prostrate themselves before him. Especially when the woman is as ridiculous as the monkey! When she reads philosophy, for instance, and translates Newton!

[VOLTAIRE *turns pale.*]

As did Émilie du Châtelet! The grand Madame du Châtelet! Did you know, gentlemen, Voltaire wouldn't be here at all, if, after eighteen years of sucking her noble and profitable tits, he couldn't stomach going to bed with her one more time—haven't you heard this, gentlemen? it is really very funny—so, he turned her over to a young lout, with his brains in his britches, to keep her happy, and he certainly *did*, because she, at forty-two, lost her senses in bliss, and got herself pregnant, pregnant, you understand—

[VOLTAIRE *rises.*]

And like the fool she was, died! *Died*, in childbirth!

VOLTAIRE [*livid*]

What, Sire? What, Sire? The memory of the woman I loved, a great lady who died in my arms, you with your vile tongue, thus attack in my presence?

FREDERICK

A monkey's whore? Why not?

VOLTAIRE

I have no sword! I have my pen! You want war? We will have it!

FREDERICK [*seizing* VOLTAIRE]

There! Will we, indeed! Now, you feel it! And you are the man who will lecture this bloodthirsty warlord! You know how kingdoms should be ruled, you preach brotherly love to mankind, but when *you* are touched, you roast your own enemies alive! You make verse like a god. You have the character of a monkey. You disgust me down to the heels of my boots! And that is the philosophical truth, anyway, you goddamned French fop.

[VOLTAIRE *moves away from him, with dignity.*]

Act III

Well, gentlemen? Converse! Talk! [FREDERICK *pulls out his snuffbox, jams snuff up his nose. He sneezes with a great convulsion and wipes his hand on his shirt. He sees* VOLTAIRE *staring at him.*] What are you looking at?

VOLTAIRE
   I shall look where I please.

FREDERICK [*after a pause, stares at the portrait*]
   What did you say?

VOLTAIRE
   I must inform Your Majesty, I shall look where I please.

FREDERICK [*Stunned by memory, he speaks softly.*]
   I must regretfully bring this enjoyable conversation to a close. It has been a great pleasure. Dinner will be served to you somewhere else. Good evening.

   [*Exeunt all but* FREDERICK. *In a moment, re-enter* VOLTAIRE.]
   Yes?

VOLTAIRE
   I have come to pay my respects to Your Majesty.

FREDERICK
   You insist, then, on this leave-taking?

VOLTAIRE
   My health and my work make it necessary, Sire.

FREDERICK
   Then I wish you a pleasant journey, monsieur.

VOLTAIRE
   Sire?

FREDERICK
   We have a few things that belong to each other. They should be returned.

VOLTAIRE

As you wish. To what does Your Majesty refer?

FREDERICK

My Chamberlain's seal. Begin with that.

VOLTAIRE

Here it is, on this ribbon around my throat. I had hoped to keep it, but, as you say, it is yours. What else?

FREDERICK

My trust. You cannot break a ribbon and return that so easily.

VOLTAIRE

Did I ever have it? You cannot trust your generals with your soldiers, your stewards with your wines, your judges with your laws, or your treasury with your people's money. If you threw a bone to a dog, you would track him down to be certain he chewed it in the prescribed manner and did not somehow deceive you.

FREDERICK

And you? You have not deceived me?

VOLTAIRE

I gave you my heart, Sire.

FREDERICK

The worst part of yourself! You should have kept that and given me the rest. You have the imagination of a sick child, who always expects too much. Now you fill yourself with disgust because the King of Prussia will not live out your ridiculous dreams.

VOLTAIRE

It is not in a dream that I see a man who pretends to be a friend, while he holds a pistol in his pocket. No dream shows me your genius poisoned by a brutality that pours gall into your soul, or this wretched pleasure you must

Act III

take in humiliating other men, a pleasure all the more disgraceful since you are elevated so far above them all, both by rank and that very imagination you now so quaintly despise! What is the reason for this black wind that destroys our friendship, and turns everything into malice? Where has it come from?

FREDERICK

From God, in whom we are pleased not to believe. I know very well that I have faults, great faults. You know I do not treat myself gently.

VOLTAIRE

Ah, Your Majesty, let that alone for now, I beg you! This grand vocation as a hero and this posture as a king have ravaged your heart, and this really is too bad, my Lord, for without your heroism and your throne, you might have been the most charming man in all the world. Good-bye, philosopher.

FREDERICK

Philosopher, good-bye.

[VOLTAIRE *bows and leaves.* FREDERICK *stares coldly ahead. The Seven Years' War begins. Enter the* CABINET *with proclamations.*]

CHANCELLOR

Aware of the feminine coalition of the empresses of Europe to invade his Kingdom and to take from him the province of Silesia, His Majesty commands the only action open to a man of honor. He declares a state of war to exist between this nation and Saxony, and Sweden, and Austria, and Russia, and France!

GENERAL

Prussians! The Empire, the continent, shake before you! The great King strikes in every direction about him, changing the face of war!

DOCTOR

With two hundred thousand soldiers, he attacks forces holding together one hundred million men!

BISHOP

Match his spirit! Equal his valor! Pray to Almighty God, and march with him, to glory!

[*The war rages.*]

GENERAL

Commanders! Military instructions from the King of Prussia. When it is difficult to gain intelligence of the enemy, seize a rich German. Force him to go to the enemy posing as a traitor. If he cannot return with the desired intelligence, burn his land, and kill his wife and children. It serves the purpose.

[*The war continues. The* CABINET *moves downstage.*]

CHANCELLOR

His ferocity is inhuman! Seven years of war! Seven years of impossible battlefields, burning cities, tortured people, dead soldiers, bloody hands, and blasted hopes!

BISHOP

The fatherland is burning now. We writhe in a holocaust of foreign invaders.

DOCTOR

Around us we face the dire hatred of all of Europe.

GENERAL

The capital has fallen. The Russian army is in Berlin. Cossacks are burning the palaces and slaughtering the people.

BISHOP

We must sue for peace! Now, in the name of God!

Act III

FREDERICK [*reciting*]
>My sorrows now outstrip my life and will,
>High praise, you gods, for savage and unending skill.
>Your scorn supreme, within this bloody cage,
>Enshrines me here, a token of your rage.

[*Enter* SOLDIER 2, *who stands waiting, holding the old* FREDERICK's *cloak, cane, and hat.*]

DOCTOR
>Majesty!

FREDERICK
>Yes?

GENERAL
>The Russian army has withdrawn!

FREDERICK
>I know.

CHANCELLOR
>That bitch, the Empress Elizabeth, is dead.

FREDERICK
>So is Voltaire.

BISHOP
>Young Peter is Czar! He sends you his greetings.

FREDERICK
>I am saved. And Voltaire, dead.

GENERAL
>Czar Peter of Holy Russia offers you the protection of his army.

FREDERICK
>Yes. Mad little Peter sends me his love. He worships me. His uniform, his personal guard, all just like mine. He

drills his soldiers in Prussian drill. But he drills cats, too! He court-martialed one once and executed it himself, on a tiny gibbet! Cats! It's perfect! Oh, God, a fool can always find a bigger fool to fall in love with him.

DOCTOR

Majesty. The Russian Army will now defend us. The Kingdom is saved.

FREDERICK

Yes, you're quite right. Saved! Voltaire is dead. Peter lives, and we are saved, again. [*To* SOLDIER 2] Did he die with the priests, as I said he would?

[SOLDIER 2 *holds out* FREDERICK's *cane, cloak, and hat.*]

SOLDIER 2

He signed an article of faith, Majesty, so he could be buried in a churchyard.

FREDERICK [*gently*]

Revolting. A ditch would have been nobler. And fitting. [*He takes his cloak and puts it over his shoulders.*] No one asks us whether we wish to be born. We are put here. We suffer, and never know why we were forced to march through life and bear such cruelty. [*He takes his hat.*] Then we sink into nothingness, still resenting the futile role we have been obliged to play on this mysterious, shabby planet. [*He takes his cane. He is the old man again.*] Voltaire. Voltaire. We are judged not by our motives but by our success. The only thing left to do is achieve it. The world will always believe the worst of us, and it is quite right. We are malevolent animals, as God made us. There is nothing worse than a man.

[*Exeunt first* FREDERICK, *then the* CABINET. *Enter the* POTSDAM GIANT, *now an old man like* FREDERICK. *He is drunk. It is the present again. Enter* FREDERICK.]

Act III

POTSDAM GIANT
>Who goes there?

FREDERICK
>The King. He must pass.

POTSDAM GIANT
>The King? No, no, the King is dead. Died forty years ago, and more. I know, I was in his service. He died, and I was thrown out. I was a young man, then. In the Royal Potsdam Guards. Maybe you remember us. We were all seven feet tall or taller. The King loved us. We were his favorites. He had us kidnapped when we were boys. From all over the world. I was from Poland. Somebody saw how tall I was, and they kidnapped me and sold me to the King of Prussia. Maybe you remember. We were famous.

FREDERICK
>I remember you very well.

POTSDAM GIANT
>What did you think of us?

FREDERICK [*sits with him*]
>You frightened me.

POTSDAM GIANT [*laughing*]
>Did we?

FREDERICK
>Yes. I did not like soldiers then. Especially soldiers seven feet tall, and I was afraid of you. I remember.

POTSDAM GIANT
>So do I! What else do I have to remember? I'll tell you the truth, it's the only thing I can remember! Seven feet tall, a soldier of the King! Bugles and straight lines, and the commands of the field. Polishing my rifle until the barrel gleamed. Scraping my bayonet until it caught the

sunlight like a mirror. All that was over forty years ago, but I can't forget it. It was so simple, you see, and good. A good life. I have been staggering around for forty years afterward, poisoning myself, trying to die. But every morning the bugle blows in my brain, I am resurrected again, I go here, go there, try to find something good to do, but all I can think about are the commands. None come. But you said you didn't like soldiers. I must be repulsive to you. All soldiers are, without commands.

FREDERICK
No. I am a soldier myself.

POTSDAM GIANT
Then you know what I'm talking about.

FREDERICK
Yes.

POTSDAM GIANT
Did you drill in the mornings? When it was fresh and the day was clear, and you could hear the commands sing in the air?

FREDERICK
Sometimes.

POTSDAM GIANT
Wasn't that wonderful? Wasn't that brave? I dream about it every night. Seventy years old, but I still dream about it. But who now will command me? To whom do I hire myself out? What wars do I serve?

FREDERICK [*touching him*]
Now, listen. The King must pass. And really, he will be very interested to see you, standing guard over his back roads all these years. He will know what happened to you, even if you do not. That you were kidnapped, and torn away from yourself, for so was he. That you were

Act III

drilled into slavery and forced to love what terrified you, until there was little room inside you for anything else. And that now, old as you are, you can never forget any of it. Neither can he, he has lived a victim just as long as you; your image is very familiar to him. And now, you will stand firm as he passes, and salute as you should—for he has his duties and his griefs, too; he is the King. He remembers you. You have never been out of his mind. Are you ready?

[FREDERICK *rises. The* POTSDAM GIANT *stares at him.*]

The King!

[*The* POTSDAM GIANT *lurches to his feet and salutes. Slowly,* FREDERICK *passes before him, as in review. They part. Exit the* POTSDAM GIANT. FREDERICK *stands to one side, waiting. Enter* SOLDIERS 1 *and* 2 *with a small coffin. They set it down and clean it.*]

SOLDIER 1
When did he start doing this?

SOLDIER 2
Years ago. He's so old, nobody remembers now.

SOLDIER 1
What was her name? Do you know?

SOLDIER 2
Frolic, I think. Yes, Frolic.

SOLDIER 1
Was she another—

SOLDIER 2
Whippet, yes. Little greyhounds, always. Delicate things. High-strung. Sensitive. You could see daylight through their skins.

SOLDIER 1
Who took care of them? Who trained them?

SOLDIER 2
Nobody. Only the King touched them. No collars, no leashes, not one harsh word. Ever. He fed them himself. He took one to bed with him every night, as long as anyone remembers. When one got sick, he acted like a maniac. When one died—well, you'll see.

SOLDIER 1
What? What will he do?

SOLDIER 2
When Lark died, he shut himself in his rooms with her body for six days. We could hear him howling from as far away as the parade ground. When we buried Solace, he took the Army right into spring maneuvers. He had cavalry jumping ditches fifty horses abreast, and he dug the trenches wider until they fell. He ran foot soldiers through gauntlets, like rats. Those maneuvers were worse than his wars. And this is the last of them. Frolic. God knows what he'll do when he sees her. That side clean? Not a spot, now.

SOLDIER 1
Not a speck.

SOLDIER 2
All right.

[*Enter* FREDERICK. *Exeunt* SOLDIERS 1 *and* 2. FREDERICK *kneels before the coffin.*]

FREDERICK
Oh, my darling. My angel. My friend. You were so young, and so beautiful. [*Pause*] Why did you leave me? [*Pause*] You were captured once by the Austrians. Did you know that? Well, you were. And I could do nothing

Act III

about it, though I would have given the universe to get you back. Then, one day, while I was buried in maps and papers, deciding this and signing that, the Austrian General sent you back. My soldiers let you into my tent, without telling me. And you came barking to me. You jumped into my arms, upsetting the papers of war. [*He weeps.*] I wept for you then, as I weep for you now. You are my only philosophy. I will be closer to you, soon.

[*He rises.* SOLDIER 1 *takes away the coffin. The other stands silently before* FREDERICK.]

Oh.

[SOLDIER 2 *escorts* FREDERICK *to his cot.*]

Thank you.

[*He lies down. Exit* SOLDIER 2. *Enter the* DOCTOR.]

DOCTOR
A short rest, Majesty. It will do wonders.

FREDERICK
Please. You know very well why I lie down now.

DOCTOR
I have watched you conquer your enemies before, when I thought you could not do it. You will do so again.

FREDERICK
Stale imagery. But would you say I have shown some physical courage in my life?

DOCTOR
You faced your fate with a heroism unequaled since the Roman Empire fell into dust. Like Death, I am a professional man. Like him, in your presence, I feel nothing but awe.

FREDERICK
  Very pleasant of you. And better imagery. Good-bye.

DOCTOR [*bows*]
  Majesty. [*To us*] When he died, his body had shrunk to the size of a child's. His fevers, sweats, and constrictions never relented. He was by surgery sexually mutilated. That he lived as long as he did was a miracle. That he died sane, incredible.

[*Exit the* DOCTOR. *Enter the* CHANCELLOR.]

FREDERICK
  Anything in the Treasury? Or have you run off with it, while I lie here, on my back?

CHANCELLOR
  The Treasury is sound. You balanced every account.

FREDERICK
  Try to keep it that way, for a week at least. Then continue to lie, with that same finesse.

CHANCELLOR
  I do not have to lie about the achievements of Frederick the Great.

FREDERICK
  I was great in no respect. I was applied, like a brush. Good-bye.

CHANCELLOR [*bows*]
  Majesty. [*To us*] He was the greatest miser, anyway, ever to sit on a throne. The sweat he wrung out of us all would have floated an Armada. When he died, the beautiful palace was empty, deserted, his so-called friends long dead, his lieutenants gone. For the funeral, there wasn't a clean shirt to be found anywhere. We had to borrow one from a valet to dress the corpse. We had to scrub the corpse for hours.

Act III

[*Exit the* CHANCELLOR. *Enter the* GENERAL.]

FREDERICK

Is there still an Army, General, or have you thrown it away?

GENERAL

Majesty, the enemy believed you had returned to the field. They faltered and fled. You are the greatest soldier who ever lived.

FREDERICK

How refreshing. Another fool, General, will come along soon and steal all our little arrows. Prevent it as long as you can. Good-bye.

GENERAL [*bows*]

Majesty. [*To us*] At the end, the Army was made up of convicts, peasants, and male harlots. Only his discipline held it together. The one escape was suicide, and many took it. He despised his own people. He destroyed an empire with his wars, and shed the blood of his fatherland all over Europe. As a soldier, I say, it was not war he waged, but fratricide. When the people heard he was dead at last, there was nothing in the streets but a tremendous feeling of relief.

[*Exit the* GENERAL. *Enter the* BISHOP, *with a Bible.*]

BISHOP

It is time, Majesty, to prepare your soul for death, and for the life to come.

FREDERICK

Put that thing away. I refuse to toss petitions into the void. You are entrusted with the details of my burial, as stated in my will. You will entomb me quietly, with no pomp or ceremony, in my garden, with my dogs. Your duty. Don't fail me.

BISHOP [*bows*]

Never, Majesty. [*To us*] We buried him, of course, with stupendous pomp and ceremony, in the crypt of the Garrison Church at Potsdam. Without his dogs. But there is one other coffin in the crypt. His father's, of course. There they lie, father and son, entombed forever.

[*Exit the* BISHOP. FREDERICK *sighs*.]

FREDERICK

The mountain is passed. We will do better.

Curtain

HOLY GHOSTS

For Edgar and Amanda Loessin

Characters

NANCY SHEDMAN
COLEMAN SHEDMAN
ROGERS CANFIELD
OBEDIAH BUCKHORN, JUNIOR
VIRGIL TIDES
ORIN HART
HOWARD RUDD
LORENA COSBURG
MRS. WALL
MURIEL BOGGS
BILLY BOGGS
THE REVEREND OBEDIAH BUCKHORN, SENIOR
CARL SPECTER
BONNIE BRIDGE
CANCER MAN

PLACE: *The rural South*
TIME: *The present; an evening in early summer*

ACT I

The interior of a one-room clapboard house located off a highway in the South. A few benches are scattered about. Some battered folding chairs are stacked against one wall. Other furniture, including an old piano, is covered with sheets and canvas. On one bench a young woman, NANCY SHEDMAN, *sits reading the Bible. By her side is an opened letter written on business stationery. A broom leans against the bench. She has interrupted her work in the house to read both the Bible and the letter. Now she is reading aloud, slowly.*

NANCY

"So then—after the Lord had spoken unto them—he was received up into heaven—and sat on the right hand of God—And they went forth, and preached everywhere—the Lord working with them—and confirming the word—with signs following. Amen." [*She stares at the Bible. Then she picks up her letter and stares at it.*] They say yes. I can go. [*She shakes her head, undecided about something.*] Oh, Lord. I know I shouldn't have written off like that. I want to stay here. With him. Don't I? Yes, Lord! Thank you, Lord!

[*She puts the business letter in the Bible, closes the Bible, and suddenly presses it fervently to her forehead. Then, briskly, she puts it down, picks up her broom, and goes back to work. She does not see a young man come quietly into the house. He watches her work. When she does see him, she lets out a cry, frightened.*]

COLEMAN
    Hello, Nancy.

NANCY
    Coleman!

COLEMAN
    Oh, you Jezebel! Where's the man?

NANCY
    He's not here, Coleman. But he will be! [*She backs away.*] He will be!

COLEMAN [*calling outside*]
    Come on in, Canfield! We got her!

NANCY
    Coleman, you can't come in here now.

COLEMAN
    I'll do anything I want, Jezebel, after what you done to me! Canfield!

NANCY [*upset*]
    Oh, *what* did I do to you, Coleman?

    [*Enter* ROGERS CANFIELD, *an old man, cautiously.*]

COLEMAN
    You know damn well. [*He moves toward her.*] I ought to knock your head off!

CANFIELD
    No violence, son! That was the understanding! I have my heart condition.

    [COLEMAN *checks himself.*]

COLEMAN
    All right. All right. [*Breathes deeply*] I promised.

NANCY
    Coleman, who's this man?

Act I

COLEMAN
    My lawyer.

NANCY
    Your what?

COLEMAN
    My lawyer, God dammit! Who's going to defend me against your, oh, your deceit, and your treachery, and your goddamned female bitchery!

CANFIELD
    Son, that kind of language won't help.

COLEMAN
    It'll help me, by God Almighty! Now, lawyer, we've tracked her down. You heard her admit there's another man. Ain't that enough for a divorce?

NANCY
    Divorce?

COLEMAN
    What else, you flaming bitch?

CANFIELD
    Well, not quite, son. It's just a little more complicated. [*To* NANCY, *with shaky charm*] Madam, allow me to ask, are you Nancy Shedman, wife to Coleman Shedman?

NANCY
    Yes, I am.

CANFIELD
    Then let me say, first, I regret the distress this meeting must cause you. Yet I feel certain we will all conduct ourselves here in a manner that can do credit to married ladies and gentlemen in an orderly and lawful civilization.

COLEMAN
    Oh, fuck that, Canfield! Get down to business!

NANCY

Oh, you are so coarse! Coarse, and just downright repulsive!

COLEMAN

Coarse, am I? Repulsive, am I? Didn't you run out of our house with a man you never saw before? Tell the truth, Nancy! You been having carnal intercourse with the son of a bitch or not?

NANCY

I have not, Coleman, been doing what you say to no man! It is your ugly eyes looking out of your ugly face that sees ugly things. I did find a friend. I have entered into a tender human relationship.

COLEMAN

She's fucking him, Canfield. It's an open confession.

NANCY

It is not! It's the laying down of an unbearable burden. [*To* CANFIELD] I can't help the mistake I made marrying this clod, who blackens every sweet thing he sees with his dirty, dusty mind.

COLEMAN

You hear how she talks to me? You hear how my wife talks to me?

CANFIELD

Yes, yes. Mrs. Shedman, would you consider discussing this other gentleman who has—ah—befriended you?

COLEMAN

That's it, Canfield! What's his name, Nancy?

NANCY

I'm not ashamed to tell you that, since he has asked me to marry him. His name is Obediah Buckhorn. He is a great preacher.

Act I

COLEMAN

I never heard of him.

NANCY [*angry*]

Oh, Coleman, you are so dumb! You can't help it, and God have mercy on you, Coleman, but you are as dumb as a ditch! You are *the* fool of creation!

COLEMAN

Hear that? The fool of creation. Well, let me tell you this, Nancy. That preacher you ran off with, he ain't going to think I'm a fool when I get my hands on him. I'm going to break his goddamned neck.

[*Enter* OBEDIAH BUCKHORN, JR. *He is a huge young man with enormous muscles. He is handsome, cheerful, and self-confident.*]

OBY

Good evening. God bless everyone here.

NANCY

Oby! [*She runs to* OBY, *throws herself into his arms.*]

COLEMAN

See what I meant, Canfield? And me not even married to her a year. I'll be damned.

OBY [*holding* NANCY *protectively*]

I hope not, Christian. I know you're Nancy's husband. You're angry now. I don't blame you for that.

COLEMAN

Wait a minute. How do you know I'm her husband? I never saw you before.

OBY

No, but I saw you, Christian. That's why she's here, with us.

COLEMAN
Us?

NANCY
I been trying to tell you, Coleman. You won't listen, as always. There's more people *involved!* I am not going—

COLEMAN
Whoever's in on it! When I get through with you—

CANFIELD
No violence, son!

OBY
There won't be. I'm not a violent man, thank God. [*He picks up a piece of metal pipe and bends it over his knee easily, smiles, tosses it away.*] I don't like to fight, Christian.

COLEMAN
Maybe not, Christian, but you sure like to run off with other men's wives. And don't call me no Christian. I'm not one. Ain't Nancy told you what I think of that?

OBY
She has. I'm giving you the benefit of the doubt.

COLEMAN
Oh, you are? Well, all right, then, Christian! I beg everybody's pardon. I'm sorry to act up. No excuse for it. This Christian stole my wife, my furniture, my family heirlooms, and my Dodge pickup truck. So praise God, Christian, what have I got to complain about?

OBY [*upset*]
Steal? Steal? [*To* NANCY] *Steal?*

NANCY
We didn't, Oby.

Act I

COLEMAN

Steal, steal, steal, he's a parrot. He must be some stud, Nancy, to make up for it. Right?

NANCY

Coleman, you are the disgust of this world. Low-down meaner than worms, you vile man. I will not talk to you further.

COLEMAN

That's why I got a lawyer. Canfield?

CANFIELD

Sensible young people. Let's sit down and talk. Save everybody's time and money, and avoid going to court. Where I haven't been in so long anyway, I could make a lot of mistakes.

NANCY

Oby, do we have time for this now? It'll just get more confused.

OBY

Whether we have time or not, I don't want anybody thinking I stole anything.

NANCY

All right, Coleman, your lawyer is trying to be civilized. I will do the same and serve coffee or tea. Which do you prefer, Mr. Canfield?

CANFIELD

Why tea, Mrs. Shedman. I thank you.

NANCY

Not at all. Oby?

OBY

Tea, please.

NANCY
    Coleman?

COLEMAN
    God damn.

NANCY
    That'll be three teas then. I got it right here.

COLEMAN
    Aw, never mind no goddamned tea party—

OBY [*firmly*]
    Sit down.

CANFIELD
    Do that, son. Just do that.

    [COLEMAN *sits, in disgust.* NANCY *fixes tea.* CANFIELD *takes out a pint bottle of whiskey.*]

    And I'll need a little of this to go with it, I'm afraid. I'm getting tired. Next thing, I'll have chest pains.

COLEMAN
    Just a little, now!

CANFIELD
    Son, if I'm to maintain my legal efficiency, not to mention my mortal life, I got to have it. It keeps the big arteries loose and clear. Now, you want a lawyer, or not?

COLEMAN
    All right, all right.

    [CANFIELD *takes a terrific snort of whiskey.*]

    Canfield! Don't knock back straight whiskey like that! You're too damn old. I don't want a lawyer dying on me!

OBY
    You need to drink whiskey, my friend?

Act I

CANFIELD
> I do. And God bless it. It loosens my heart.

OBY
> Sorry to hear you say that. My daddy would be, too. A man with heart trouble needs religion and healthy food, not whiskey. I eat soybeans and wheat protein. And look at me.
>
> [*Enter a young boy,* VIRGIL TIDES. *He carries a wooden box. It is marked "Shotgun Shells."*]

NANCY
> Hello, Virgil.

VIRGIL
> Hidy. I got them.

OBY
> Set them down over there, Virgil. Out of the way.

NANCY
> Want some tea?

VIRGIL
> No, m'am. [*He sets the box very carefully against one wall, and goes out.*]

COLEMAN
> What the hell kind of strange kid was that?

NANCY
> A dear friend, Coleman. Not some kid Here's boneset tea for everybody. And sugar. And sugar spoons.

COLEMAN
> My great-grandmother's silver sugar spoons! Nancy, you stole every single thing of value right out of our house!

NANCY
> Nobody stole nothing, Coleman!

CANFIELD
Now, young married people—

COLEMAN
That was just plain wrong!

CANFIELD
You see, the way we do this—

NANCY
It was a fair division of property!

COLEMAN
The hell it was!

CANFIELD
If you'll just listen in an orderly—

NANCY
And I earned every stick of it twenty times over!

COLEMAN
And I'm getting every stick of it back!

CANFIELD
There has to be some kind—

NANCY
Not one spoon! Not one shred of nothing, Coleman!

COLEMAN
All of it, Nancy! All of it!

CANFIELD
Hold it, youth! Just hold it!

[*They stop.*]

Whew. There's a better way to do this. Believe me. [*To* COLEMAN] Client, do you really want a divorce?

COLEMAN
I do.

Act I

CANFIELD
   Mrs. Shedman, do you want a divorce?

NANCY
   If he does. But I'm not giving him back—

COLEMAN
   Oh, yes you are!

CANFIELD
   That comes later! Whew. First, we got to sort out the grounds for this action. Who did what to who and how, and so on.

COLEMAN
   You sure you know what you're doing?

CANFIELD
   Just trust me, son. Now, Mrs. Shedman—

NANCY
   Call me Nancy.

CANFIELD
   Now, Nancy—

COLEMAN
   Canfield, whose side you on here, anyhow?

NANCY
   Stop fighting with your own lawyer!

COLEMAN
   I'm not! I'm just making damn sure you don't—

CANFIELD
   Listen, youth! Just listen. We have to sort it out. Like this, now. [*He gets up. He takes a deep breath.*] My name is Rogers Canfield.

COLEMAN
   I know that!

NANCY
> Hush!

CANFIELD
> Attorney at Law. In retirement, for my health. I am a widower.

COLEMAN
> What the hell does that have to do—

NANCY
> Just listen, Coleman!

CANFIELD
> Procedure, son. Calm procedure. Thank you, Nancy.

NANCY
> Don't mention it.

COLEMAN
> Aw, my God.

CANFIELD
> I live with my daughter, who never married. In a little house. See, I've established these facts. Now, this morning I was sitting on the porch, with nothing to do, looking at the road. Young Shedman came to see me. Clear so far?

NANCY
> Yes, indeed.

COLEMAN
> Yes, yes!

CANFIELD
> He asked me if I knew a lawyer who could help him in his marital distress. I said I might. See how the facts can fall? Gently, and one at a time?

NANCY
> I understand perfectly.

Act I

COLEMAN
So do I, so do I.

CANFIELD
Good. We're making progress. Mr. Shedman told me he didn't have much in the way of a fee. About that time, my daughter came out of the house, mad at me over something or other, said so, and went back in. I said, "Mr. Shedman, get me off this porch today, and I'm yours." We made a deal. I'm out of legal retirement to serve him faithfully. That understood?

NANCY
Absolutely.

COLEMAN
Of course! Of course!

CANFIELD
Then you see how easy and gentle it can go. It's so simple. Just try it my way, young married people.

COLEMAN
Okay. Fair enough. You first, Nancy.

NANCY
No, you first, Coleman.

COLEMAN
Nancy—

NANCY
You started this action, Coleman!

CANFIELD
She has a point, son.

COLEMAN
Fine. I'll do it. I mean to be fair, Nancy, and right and honorable, and speak the truth.

CANFIELD
> And that's a point for you.

NANCY
> I'm listening.

CANFIELD
> You see, we're doing all right. Son?

> [COLEMAN *gets up. He imitates* CANFIELD.]

COLEMAN
> My name is Coleman Hannibal Shedman, Jr. I own and manage—

> [*Enter* VIRGIL *with another box.* COLEMAN *stares at him. He sets it carefully next to the first one, and exits.*]

NANCY
> He'll be in and out, Coleman. Don't worry about him.

COLEMAN
> I own and manage the Shedman Fish Farm, left me by my father when he died. I breed the finest lake stock in the South. It was a good life until one year ago, when, like a fool, I wanted to get married. I met this woman, who said she loved me. But she didn't love me, not even from the very beginning!

> [*As* COLEMAN *talks,* NANCY *shows signs of acute distress. It is difficult for her to listen without breaking in.*]

> Because, on our honeymoon, which I planned and planned to the last detail to please her, I took her all the way to Virginia! To camp there at beautiful Hungry Mother State Park! I bought us a brand new tent, planning for us to swim in the beautiful lake, and fish together, and I'd show her how to cook out, and then watch the sunset with my loving wife. But wrong again, Coleman. Because all she could say was, Hungry Mother is a stupid name

Act I

for a State Park, and a miserable place for a Christian honeymoon, picking my plans all to pieces bit by bit, until there wasn't nothing left of what I tried to do for us but the inside of that tent, as black as blackest night. And it was more of the same almost for one whole year, until one week ago.

NANCY

All right, all right now.

COLEMAN

I come home that night. I was emotional, upset, full of misguided love. I took Nancy tenderly in my arms, and tried to tell her how much I cared—

NANCY

Oh, my God.

COLEMAN

But I was tired! Working and slaving to support my wife at the fish farm. I fell asleep. And when I woke up the next morning, wife, furniture, family heirlooms, and my Dodge pickup truck, gone. Gone! In their place, a little note. "Dear Coleman. Last night I met a real man. Yours truly, Nancy." Well, all right. But God damn it, I want all my family furniture, and my family heirlooms, and my pickup truck, and a divorce! My wife and Mr. Soy Bean can have each other, I'll live with Daddy's fish! They treat me better than she ever did! [*He sits down.*]

NANCY [*jumping up*]

Oh boy, Coleman! Oh boy, Coleman!

CANFIELD

Gently, now, sensible married people! Gently.

NANCY

My name may be Nancy Shedman, but I'm not yours no more, Coleman, you frog. Not in no way, shape, or form!

COLEMAN

Is that a goddamned promise?

NANCY

It certainly is, and has been, since that same night you have described out of the folly of your twisted mouth.

COLEMAN

Hear that? Twisted mouth.

NANCY

Because a lot more happened that night than you'll admit, Coleman, you horse-faced rat and rodent, you!

COLEMAN

Horse-faced rat and rodent. Hear that?

CANFIELD

Now, gently, sensible young—

NANCY

You come home, all right. Looking like you always do, puffed up mad at the world, and me in it. You weren't full of misguided love, you were full of beer and whiskey! You wouldn't say a word. Just mope around, and mope around, and then, *boom!* All of a sudden grabbing me. Hauling me down on the sofa, like a sack of potatoes. Starting in on me until I myself, in spite of myself, was swept with carnal desire. When I finally managed to get my clothes decently off, you pawing and clutching, and finally got my desires decently ready for you, I said so. Because I wanted you, Coleman, because I want a *baby*, Coleman, a *baby*, and said so! Then, you climbing on top of me on that old sofa and just hanging there. Then passing out! Out, just plain out, *boom!* Like that. Me rolling humiliated out from under you, and letting you flop, *boom!* your big stuffed head going down like a rock, hitting the coffee table, *boom!* like that, splitting your lip, and me wishing you'd split your brains and broke your neck! Oh, Coleman, oh, Coleman! You don't know what it's like, to be a mortified wife. I felt so bad. Dear Jesus, I prayed, give me a sign. And about that time, you snorted, and rolled over on your back on the floor, *flop!* like that, with your pants down and that thing of yours sleeping just like you, *flop!* F-l-o-p, *flop!*

[*Listening to this,* COLEMAN *has been going crazy. Now he sees a large, rough-looking man,* ORIN HART, *enter.* ORIN *is looking anxiously for someone he missed on the way, hoped would be there, and isn't. Disappointed, he sits alone on a bench.*]

COLEMAN
Who's that man?

NANCY
Oh, hush! There I was, naked in my own living room, with my husband passed out on the floor. Again. Because that's what always happens, since that campfire honeymoon of his. Instead of decent married relations, it's him get drunk, me want a baby, *boom!* and *flop!* It was such a mess. I wanted to die. I hadn't even noticed he'd left the front door open. Somebody was there. I turned around, crying. It was Oby.

COLEMAN
Doing what, preacher? Whacking off?

OBY
Now, hold on—

NANCY
Asking me politely, Coleman, if I had a kitchen match. So he could light his campfire down by the river. So understanding and polite about the fact I didn't have my clothes on, so gentle and kindly faced.

COLEMAN

He ain't kindly faced. He ain't nothing faced. He's so goddamned dumb, nothing registers there at all.

NANCY

I register there! Your wife registers there, and likes it a lot. [*To* CANFIELD] Oby waited while I put on my clothes. I got his matches. And I went with him to his campfire. And it was so different. A different campfire from any of yours, Coleman. I told Oby everything. He understood. And he told me things, about life, and Jesus our Lord, and the Bible—things I sure never heard before anywhere. And he took me in his manly arms, and said a prayer in my ear, and kissed me. And then, oh! what a difference, between [*pointing at* OBY] day and [*pointing at* COLEMAN] night!

[*Another tough-looking man,* HOWARD RUDD, *enters. He is not as big as* ORIN, *but he is just as rough.*]

OBY [*to* HOWARD]

Sit down anywheres. We'll be through in no time.

HOWARD [*distracted*]

Is Orin here?

[ORIN *and* HOWARD *see each other. They quickly embrace.*]

ORIN

I thought you wasn't coming!

HOWARD

I waited half an hour at the poolroom!

ORIN

Poolroom? I thought you said meet here!

HOWARD

No, no, we were supposed to meet here and go there later!

ORIN
   Who said that?

HOWARD
   You did.

ORIN
   No, I didn't. What I said was—

HOWARD
   Well, never mind. I'm sorry if I messed up.

ORIN
   No, I did. Just so you're here.

HOWARD
   I am.

ORIN
   It's all right, then. Everything's all **right**.

   [*They embrace. A pale, drab, middle-aged lady,* LORENA COSBURG, *enters timidly.*]

LORENA
   Oh, I'm sorry! I thought there was a church service in here. I don't mean to intrude. [*She turns to go.*]

OBY
   You're not intruding, m'am. Come right in and sit down. It'll begin shortly.

COLEMAN
   Wait a minute. Them two men are hugging and kissing each other back there.

NANCY
   Just let me finish. I came back to the house with Oby, happy for the first time in my woman's life. With you, still passed out on the floor. I said, "Listen, Oby, I have earned freedom, a fair division of furniture, and trans-

portation, too." So we loaded everything I wanted over your head, out the door, and put it in your filthy old truck, and drove off. To here. Where I stand now, defying you, Coleman, you dog. By the way, I sold your truck.

[*A large woman named* MRS. WALL *enters impressively. She waves to* NANCY.]

NANCY
  Hidy.

MRS. WALL
  Hello, Nancy. You sweet thing. Praise the Lord.

COLEMAN
  Now who, for God's sake, is that?

NANCY
  Mrs. Wall.

COLEMAN
  Mrs. who?

MRS. WALL
  Wall! Wall!

COLEMAN
  Two men hugging each other, and a woman named Wall.

[MRS. WALL *removes the sheet covering a battered upright piano. She settles herself there.*]

NANCY
  She's a sweet Christian companion and friend. Never you mind about her name. So, Mr. Canfield, that is my story. Do you understand everything now?

CANFIELD
  I fear I am beginning to, yes.

COLEMAN [*to* OBY]
  All right, Soy Bean. Your turn.

Act I

OBY
> Me?

COLEMAN
> We get to hear your story of what happened on that fateful night. [*Looks at the people*] All fifty of us, or however the hell many people we got in here now. O my God!

> [*A young man,* BILLY BOGGS, *with a guitar, enters. With him is his young wife,* MURIEL, *a baby in her arms.*]

MURIEL
> Hey, Nancy.

NANCY
> Muriel! You brought the baby!

MURIEL
> I sure did!

NANCY [*to the baby*]
> Why, he's just the sweetest thing! Hey, there! Hey, honey! Whoo-hoo! Buba-buba-boo! Oh, Lord, Muriel, he's nice.

MURIEL
> Yes, he is.

> [BILLY *hits a note on* MRS. WALL's *piano, and tunes one string of his guitar.* MRS. WALL *joins* NANCY *and* MURIEL, *who are looking at the baby.*]

BILLY [*to* COLEMAN]
> Hi. [*He moves away, tuning his guitar.*]

COLEMAN
> Elvis Presley. My God. Hey, Soy Bean!

> [*Smiling, at ease,* OBY *takes his turn.*]

OBY
> You want to hear my story, here it is, cross my heart and

hope to die. [*To* CANFIELD] It started when I got laid off my full-time job at the Skyrocket Bowling Alley. Couldn't get along with the manager. I went up in the mountains to think about it, and fish, and pray. I was camping by Caesar's Creek, just above Stone Mountain River. I went to cook my trout, but I'd run out of matches. I'd seen this little house up by the road. I went and looked, and there was a light on inside. The front door was open. I looked in. There, without any clothes on, was a fine young lady. [OBY *smiles, and spreads his hands. He appreciates the absurdity of the occasion.*] I said, "Ah, hello. You got a match?" And she said maybe she did. When I told her what I wanted it for, she said if I could wait until she put some clothes on, she'd not only give me a box of matches, she'd come down and cook my trout for me. And she did. [*To* COLEMAN] And told me about you.

COLEMAN
What about me, Soy Bean?

OBY
Enough. You want to know why she likes my campfire better than yours? Because I know that God Himself is always the other person around any fire. Any fire. She understands that now, too. [*To* CANFIELD *again*] She asked me what to do about her husband. I said, "Go ask my daddy. He preaches about men and women all the time. He knows more than I do." She said that sounded like a good idea. She had a pickup truck and some furniture she wanted to take with her. Fine. Well, Daddy liked her right off. So much, he offered her the back room over the kitchen in our house for as long as she wants. Folks often stay with us from time to time. Ask around, lawyer. You will find we are respected Christian people. Nothing wrong has been done. And, since then, I've been looking for a steady job. Today, I got one. I can't wait to tell

Act I

my daddy about it. [*Smiling with anticipation, he sits down.*]

COLEMAN

How about it, Canfield? Read between the lines. If that ain't enough for a divorce, what is?

[*Sounds of guitar, piano chords. Moving about, friendly, but not gushing, the people chat with each other. They are at ease, but it is evident they are all here for a serious purpose.*]

CANFIELD

My goodness. Just look at all these people.

COLEMAN

Listen, Oby. Are you trying to tell me that, instead of having carnal relations with my wife, when she was wide open, if you can pardon the expression, you took her instead to see your daddy?

OBY

That's right.

COLEMAN

Then what the hell are you doing, pimping for your daddy?

NANCY

Coleman—

COLEMAN

And what kind of grown-up man lives with his daddy, anyhow? Great God Almighty, if my old man and me lived in the same house one day after I hit sixteen, they'd a buried the both of us.

NANCY

Coleman—

COLEMAN [*to* OBY]
   But not you. You live with Daddy.

NANCY
   Coleman—

COLEMAN [*to* NANCY]
   And so do you, now! When you marry him, you still gonna live with Daddy?

NANCY
   Coleman—

COLEMAN
   Well, what is it, Nancy? Speak up!

NANCY
   Coleman, you are the one who's insisted all this time I am going to marry Oby.

COLEMAN
   Huh?

NANCY
   I'm not.

COLEMAN
   Huh?

NANCY
   Oby is my dear friend and brother in the Lord, but he is not my happiness. He brought me to it, but he is not the thing itself.

COLEMAN
   Wait a minute. You said you was going to marry Obediah Buckhorn.

NANCY
   Yes. Obediah Buckhorn, Senior.

Act I

OBY [*smiling*]
>Daddy.

COLEMAN
>*Daddy?* You marrying his *daddy?*

NANCY
>Yes! Finally, Coleman, whew! That's it!

COLEMAN
>Well, Go-a-odd-damn! Daddy, eh? Canfield, my fine young wife left me for Daddy. Well, where is he? Let's all have a look at Daddy. Daddy! Yoo-hoo! Daddy? Where in hell is he, anyhow?

>[*Enter the* REVEREND OBEDIAH BUCKHORN, SR.]

REVEREND BUCKHORN
>Right here. God bless you, son.

COLEMAN
>Him?

NANCY
>Him. [*She goes to the* REVEREND BUCKHORN *and stands beside him.*] At last, you got here. It's my husband. [*To* COLEMAN] The Reverend Buckhorn will take care of everything now, Coleman.

COLEMAN
>She wants to marry this old man? Jesus Christ! [*To* REVEREND BUCKHORN] Well, Daddy, I can put your ass in jail. For it seems you and your idjit son here have stole my wife.

REVEREND BUCKHORN [*after a pause, calmly*]
>I can see you mean to test me, son.

COLEMAN
>And fucking how. This is my lawyer, and we got you dead to rights.

REVEREND BUCKHORN
> I understand how you must feel. Life is hard.

COLEMAN
> You hear that son of a bitch say that to me? I'm gonna—

CANFIELD
> Son! No violence!

REVEREND BUCKHORN
> But your wife came to us of her own free will. And suffering, because of you. [*To* NANCY] And her own ignorance.

NANCY [*head bowed*]
> Yes, Lord.

REVEREND BUCKHORN
> All your questions, Mr. Shedman, will be answered. But we have a service to the Lord God to celebrate here tonight, and everything else must wait upon that. You will know everything you want to know—*after* the worship. Excuse me. [*He brushes past* COLEMAN *and kisses* OBY *fondly, then* NANCY *affectionately, but with a gleam in his eye, too. Then he moves away, welcoming the others, who are all waiting to greet him.*]

COLEMAN
> Lawyer! What are we going to do about it?

CANFIELD
> Well—

[*Enter* CARL SPECTER. *He is a very strange, raw-boned country man. He is full of something he has to say. He sees* COLEMAN, *someone new, and goes to him, talking.*]

CARL
> She come into my life from nowhere, don't you see? I found her in the city dump, dying in a shoebox, with all her dead little brothers and sisters around her. But she

Act I

was still alive. I took her home. I fed her cornbread and milk. And she lived. [*He nods at* COLEMAN, *having said something tremendous.*] She lived!

[*He turns to the others, who nod and make him a part of them, protectively.* COLEMAN *shakes his head.*]

COLEMAN
What was *he* talking about?

NANCY
About his phantom setter. That's Carl Specter, talking about his phantom setter.

COLEMAN
His what?

NANCY
A bird dog, Coleman, who died. He's a man haunted by his dog. Can't you understand that?

COLEMAN
Well, of course, Nancy. Sure. Hell, yes.

NANCY
Coleman, since I left you and came to live with Reverend Buckhorn, I see how limited you really are. You can't tolerate nothing in the slightest human way unusual. You have got a lot to learn.

[*Enter* BONNIE BRIDGE, *once a beautiful woman. She is practical, efficient, and cheerful.*]

BONNIE
How are you, Nancy?

NANCY
Fine, Bonnie. How're you?

BONNIE
Doing all right, praise the Lord. [*To* COLEMAN *and* CAN-FIELD] Hello. Welcome to our church. If you could give me your names, I'll see that you're properly introduced

to everyone before we begin. [*To* COLEMAN] What's your name, young man? Don't be shy.

COLEMAN
God damn it, Nancy.

BONNIE [*understanding*]
Oh, Nancy, it's your husband.

NANCY
I'm afraid so.

BONNIE
I should have known. [*To* COLEMAN] You're not here for church, then.

COLEMAN
I'm here for a divorce. This is my lawyer.

CANFIELD [*quickly extending his hand*]
My name is Rogers Canfield. Very pleased to meet you.

BONNIE
Mine is Bonnie Bridge. God bless you, sir.

CANFIELD
Thank you. God bless you, too.

[*She smiles at* CANFIELD, *and moves away to other people.* CANFIELD *stares after her.*]

COLEMAN
Canfield!

NANCY
Mr. Canfield, can we finish, please?

CANFIELD
Well. [*To* COLEMAN] I doubt if you could prove adultery, now. [*To* NANCY] But if the wife admits desertion, the husband does have grounds for divorce, and is entitled to all his property.

Act I

NANCY

Wait a minute! Who admits desertion? I left this man by the right of suffering. I had to find some decent joy and beauty in my life. Every woman has a right to that. I don't owe this fool a thing more than what he owes me: one wasted year of our lives! I'm not giving him back nothing!

COLEMAN

That's what you think, Nancy.

NANCY

That's what I know, Coleman. Now you just get out of here. We've given you all the time we can.

REVEREND BUCKHORN

I think we're ready, now. Have you finished your talk?

OBY

Yes, sir.

NANCY

Yes, sir.

REVEREND BUCKHORN

Good. Is Cancer Man here yet?

OBY

No, sir.

REVEREND BUCKHORN

We'll wait then, a few minutes. I wouldn't want to start without him. [*He moves away again.*]

COLEMAN

Cancer Man?

NANCY

Yes, Coleman.

COLEMAN

Cancer Man?

NANCY
> Yes, yes! Can't you understand English? A man who has cancer. He comes here because it helps him. He don't have no place else to go.

COLEMAN
> If he has cancer, why doesn't he go to a hospital?

NANCY
> Coleman, you don't know what you're talking about.

COLEMAN [*hurt*]
> Oh, I don't? Didn't Mama die of it when I was a boy? And didn't I take my daddy to the hospital with it not two years ago?

NANCY
> Yes. I forgot. I'm sorry.

COLEMAN
> Didn't they waste away to nothing? Didn't I watch Daddy die, not even knowing who I was? His own son?
>
> [*Enter* CANCER MAN. *He is a sick man in late middle age. The sight of him reminds* COLEMAN *of his father, and it frightens him.*]

CANCER MAN
> Hidy.

REVEREND BUCKHORN
> Hello, Cancer Man. We been waiting for you.

CANCER MAN
> Have you? Waiting for me? God bless you for that. What would we do, if we couldn't come to church? [*He sees* COLEMAN. *He holds out a hand to him.*] Hello, son.

COLEMAN [*hushed*]
> You got cancer?

Act I

CANCER MAN [*simply*]
>Yes.

[COLEMAN *turns away from him abruptly.*]

REVEREND BUCKHORN
>Now, friends. Let's start the worship. Begin.

[*The people move quickly now.* MRS. WALL *plays "Amazing Grace," and they sing it heartily as they change the room about. A table is brought to the middle of the room. It becomes an altar. On it is placed a rough wooden cross. A mason jar of cloudy liquid is placed very carefully by the cross. The wooden boxes are put before the altar. A large sign goes up:*]

| AMALGAMATION |
| HOLINESS |
| CHURCH OF GOD |
| WITH SIGNS |
| FOLLOWING |

While this is happening, COLEMAN *follows* NANCY, *who helps with the setting up of the church.*]

COLEMAN
>Wait a minute, Nancy! What about the divorce? What about my property? What about this old man you're going to marry? You lost your mind? Bunch of lunatics in here—two truck drivers hugging and kissing each other, another man talking to a dead dog, another man dancing around saying he's got cancer? What kind of religion is this, anyhow? Nancy, what's happened to you? Nancy?

[*Nobody pays him any attention. They are all cheerfully singing "Amazing Grace" and getting ready for the service.*]

CONGREGATION [*singing*]
>Amazing grace! how sweet the sound
>That saved a wretch like me!
>I once was lost, but now am found,
>Was blind, but now I see.
>
>'Twas grace that taught my heart to fear,
>And grace my fears relieved;
>How precious did that grace appear,
>The hour I first believed!
>
>Through many dangers, toils, and snares,
>I have already come;
>'Tis grace hath brought me safe thus far,
>And grace will lead me home.
>
>When we've been there ten thousand years,
>Bright shining as the sun,
>We've no less days to sing God's praise,
>Than when we first begun.
>
>Amazing grace! how sweet the sound
>That saved a wretch like me!
>I once was lost, but now am found,
>Was blind, but now I see.

[*They settle. Crude lights have been turned on. There is no formal arrangement of the* CONGREGATION. *They sit scattered about the room. In front of the altar, however, a space is left open.*]

REVEREND BUCKHORN
>Now, folks. Before anything else, it is I myself must declare myself here to you! I would hold nothing back!

CONGREGATION
>Amen, brother.

COLEMAN
>A-fucking men, and how, brother.

REVEREND BUCKHORN [*pauses and takes a deep breath*]
You all do know the sunshine that has come into my life. This young and tender maiden—

COLEMAN
Maiden? Hoo!

REVEREND BUCKHORN [*pauses and takes a deep breath*]
Who came to me lost and forlorn, ravaged by the brutality and the squalor of godless wedlock, her lovely womanly—

COLEMAN
Wedlock is right, brother. Wait till it snaps on you.

REVEREND BUCKHORN [*pauses and takes a deep breath*]
Her lovely womanly spirit crushed, her gentle nature defiled, her trusting heart broken—

COLEMAN
And pissed off, in the bargain.

REVEREND BUCKHORN [*grinding his teeth*]
Came here to me, and to our church, and asked us for help, for guidance, for love and faith. And you gave, and I gave—

COLEMAN
And she gave—

REVEREND BUCKHORN [*grinding his teeth*]
And she was healed! Made whole! Sound! Radiant with the spirit of the Lord! Is this ary kind of lie? Speak, little Nancy! Speak the truth!

NANCY [*simply, sincerely*]
I was lost, but now am found. Was blind, but now I see. You have given me back my life.

REVEREND BUCKHORN
Thank you for that. [*To the* CONGREGATION] And it is no

secret here, that my feelings for this girl have become, in the way of mortal men, matrimonial. Her youth and sunshine for me, my strength and experience for her.

COLEMAN
God damn.

REVEREND BUCKHORN
Here is her husband, come cursing amongst us. You see the man. With rage, tight as a tick. Now, Mr. Shedman, you may not believe this, but everybody here comprehends your extreme married misery. Including me. Nobody belittles it. Including me. As soon as I can, when service is over, I will have everything out with you. But first things come first. Till church is over, you are our friend and guest. We beg you, stay, and be welcome! [*To* CANFIELD] And you are welcome, too. [*To the* CONGREGATION] Isn't that right?

CONGREGATION
Why, yes. It certainly is. Yes, indeed. Welcome, friends.

CANFIELD
That's very decent of you. Much obliged. [*To* COLEMAN] Have a seat, son.

COLEMAN
What, listen to this?

CANFIELD
You have to. Don't you want your settlement? Your property back?

COLEMAN
Oh, yeah. Damn right I do. Okay.

[*Music. Chords on the piano, from the electric guitar. Perhaps a harmonica, a tambourine. Led by* BILLY *and* MRS. WALL, *they supply their own music very well.*]

Act I

CANFIELD
> Just be patient.

COLEMAN
> Oh, sure. [*He slips the whiskey bottle from* CANFIELD'*s pocket, and takes a quick drink.*] Want some?

CANFIELD
> No, thanks.

COLEMAN
> Huh?

CANFIELD
> Put that away, son. We're in church.

COLEMAN
> What about your heart condition?

CANFIELD
> I'll chance it. Now, hush up.
>
> [*They are seated to one side.* REVEREND BUCKHORN *is now at his lectern, listening to the music.*]

REVEREND BUCKHORN [*easily*]
> Well, what is real religion? One thing I know, it don't have no beginning, and it don't have no end. It is happening all the time, and tonight I hope it will happen to us. [*He listens, and smiles.*] That sounds good, Billy. Mrs. Wall. I hope we have good music tonight, to the Glory of God. I think we will. Mr. Hart. Mr. Rudd. Carl. God bless all of you, my friends. [*He turns to* BONNIE.] Miss Bridge?

BONNIE [*making announcements*]
> Friends, the Kiley Haines family were burned out of their house last night. They weren't hurt, but their clothes went up with everything else. [*Holding a piece of paper*] I have the children's sizes here. If you'll look at them

later on, and bring in what you can, I'll see they get it.

[*The* CONGREGATION *is responsive.*]

We have three new faces with us tonight. First of all—where are you? [*Looks about*] Oh, there you are. Come on out. A new friend, Mrs. Lorena Cosburg.

[LORENA *steps shyly forward.*]

CONGREGATION
Welcome. Hidy.

LORENA
Hello. [*She moves back quickly.*]

BONNIE
This gentleman is Mr. Coleman Shedman. He is Nancy's husband.

CONGREGATION
Welcome. Hidy.

COLEMAN [*a mock bow*]
Oh, how do you do?

BONNIE
And last, but certainly not least, a distinguished lawyer, Mr. Rogers Canfield.

CONGREGATION
Welcome. Hidy.

CANFIELD [*very pleased, smiling at* BONNIE]
I'm happy to be here.

BONNIE [*smiling back*]
And I have the latest about Gilbert Letty. He's out of the hospital. He's home now, with Martha. He's still in pain, but not in agony like he was. He'd welcome visits from comforting friends. And Reverend Buckhorn, may I say this?

Act I

REVEREND BUCKHORN
Of course.

BONNIE
You all know what happened to me here. How sick I was over it for so long. Let me tell you, I appreciated your visits and your prayers. I know now how the sick and the needy feel. And—oh, Lord—now I want to pray!

REVEREND BUCKHORN
Then do.

BONNIE [*praying aloud, fervently*]
Oh, Lord Jesus, I was so sick! I wanted to die so many times, and you heard my prayers and brought my friends to help me, and so, Lord, I pray now that you will send health and mercy to Gilbert Letty and his wife and children! And to all the sick and needy people in this world!

[*The others join her, each with his own prayer. In a moment, the* CONGREGATION, *many on their knees, is praying aloud with real passion for the afflicted. With a look at* COLEMAN, NANCY *falls to her knees and prays for him.*]

NANCY
Oh, Lord! Let me pray to you right now for my husband, Coleman! Forgive my evil thoughts against him! You know I can't stand him anymore, and he is a terrible mess, but maybe he can't help that, Lord, and I pray that you will come into his life and do him some good and show him the way! Amen, Lord Jesus!

[*With another look, she gets up and walks to* OBY. *The prayers, a few at a time, end. When they are all quite finished,* REVEREND BUCKHORN *speaks again.*]

REVEREND BUCKHORN
Now folks, I see Muriel and Billy Boggs there with some good news. Billy?

[BILLY *gets up, a little reluctantly.*]

BILLY

Well, we had the baby, as you know. She's got it with her. Muriel?

[*His young wife stands up, happy. She holds her baby, who has been nursing at her breast, in public.*]

MURIEL

He's only three weeks old. I wanted to bring him here quick as I could. Edward William Boggs. Billy has nicknamed him Wrinkle. That's because the first day we had him home, Billy didn't see him where I had him under a bedsheet, and almost sat on him. He said he looked like just another wrinkle in the sheets. And that's what he was. You all know we never meant to have him this fast. But we're happy about it, anyhow. Ain't we, Billy?

BILLY

Yeah.

MURIEL

He already has a godmother. Elrita Moss, who won't come here, I'm sorry to say. But he needs a godfather, for the years ahead. [*She goes to* CANCER MAN.] Will you do that for us? I believe you will get well and live for many years. He might need somebody like you, who is good and wise.

CANCER MAN

You people here. You are the best things in the world to me. [*Moved, he holds up his hands to take the baby, but very shyly.*]

MURIEL

Here. Don't be afraid to hold him. You won't scare him. He'll know you love him.

[CANCER MAN *takes the baby in his arms.*]

Act I

CANCER MAN
>I thank you, Lord Jesus. Little boy, I will stand by you, as long as I live. Bless you, child. All the days of your sweet young life.

REVEREND BUCKHORN
>What a fine thing. You know, Jesus was a baby like this, once. How we love that. Baby Jesus. Mrs. Wall, play us some Baby Jesus music. Billy, you proud daddy. Sing, friends.

>[MRS. WALL *plays "Fairest Lord Jesus." The people gather around* MURIEL *and sing it to the baby, and to her.* COLEMAN *stares at them, shaking his head.*]

COLEMAN
>Canfield, there is something wrong about these people. I just feel it.

CONGREGATION [*singing gently*]
>>Fairest Lord Jesus, ruler of all nature,
>>O Thou of God and man the son,
>>Thee will I cherish, Thee will I honor,
>>Thou, my soul's glory, joy, and crown.

COLEMAN
>I mean, they're not all right in the head. [*Looks around*] And this place. I mean, what kind of church is this?

CONGREGATION [*singing*]
>>Fair is the sunshine, fairer still the moonlight,
>>And all the twinkling, starry host.
>>Jesus shines brighter, Jesus shines purer,
>>Than all the angels heav'n can boast.

COLEMAN
>What are they doing up there, pretending that damn baby is Jesus? I tell you, something is dead wrong about this whole thing.

[*The hymn is sung to its end.* CANCER MAN *approaches* COLEMAN.]

CANCER MAN
Son?

COLEMAN
Oh, my God.

CANCER MAN
Don't you want to see the baby?

COLEMAN
No, I don't.

CANCER MAN
Why not? Pretty child. Don't you like children?

COLEMAN
What business is that of yours? What do you care if I like children or not?

CANCER MAN
I like you. I want to be your friend.

COLEMAN
Well, thank you, but I'm not interested. Look, it's too bad you're sick.

CANCER MAN
Don't worry about it. I don't.

COLEMAN
Of course not. Will you just please leave me alone?

CANCER MAN
All right. I am sorry I have troubled you.

[CANCER MAN *goes back to the others.* COLEMAN *sees* CANFIELD *looking at him with disapproval.*]

COLEMAN
What are you looking at?

Act I

CANFIELD

Nothing, son.

COLEMAN

By God, I don't see why everybody has to call me son around here. [*He steps to the center of the room.*] And I've had about enough of this! Nancy, there ain't nothing more happening in here until we get through! You can sing hymns till hell freezes over. I don't care! You can marry Oby, Daddy, or the milkman. I don't care! [*He looks about, sees the boxes in front of the table, marches over and sits on them.*] But I ain't waiting no longer. I'm here to get what's coming to me, and till I do, I'm gonna sit right here and yell about it! Come on, Nancy! My furniture, my family heirlooms, and a new pickup truck! Until that's settled, here I sit!

NANCY

Well, I wouldn't sit on them boxes, Coleman, if I were you.

COLEMAN

Oh, you wouldn't, would you? [*He sits there. He kicks them.*]

NANCY

And I wouldn't kick them like that, neither.

COLEMAN

Oh, yeah? Well, who's going to stop me? [*He kicks the boxes hard.*]

NANCY

Keep on kicking. You'll find out.

[COLEMAN *kicks the boxes and bounces on top of them, in a tantrum. Suddenly, from inside the boxes comes an unmistakable sound—the electrifying thrushing crackle of a rattlesnake.* COLEMAN *rockets up off the boxes. He looks through a crack in the side of one.*]

COLEMAN

Snakes! Jesus Christ! [*He looks again. Everybody watches him in a great silence.*] There's rattlesnakes in these boxes! Diamond goddamned backed rattlesnakes! And copperheads! Deadly serpents! They're poison. They'll kill you!

[*The* CONGREGATION *stares at* COLEMAN *and his discovery, saying not a word.*]

What are they doing in—[*Pause. Silence. Realization*] My God. You're Pentecostal Church Snakehandlers. [COLEMAN *stares at the worshipers of Amalgamation Church. The worshipers stare at* COLEMAN.]

Curtain

ACT II

As before.

COLEMAN
Pentecostal Church of God Snakehandlers. Maniacs, Canfield. [*To* REVEREND BUCKHORN] You pick up them snakes? Hold them in your hands?

REVEREND BUCKHORN
That has been known to happen.

COLEMAN
And you jump all around, and praise Jesus with rattlesnakes?

NANCY
Coleman, you're getting it wrong, as usual.

COLEMAN
Well, what's the trick? There's got to be one. You drug them snakes? Or you milk them first? Or what?

NANCY
Coleman, they are the way God made them. Full of speed, fangs, and poison death. But that ain't the point.

COLEMAN
Oh, don't tell me those— [*pause*] wait a minute. I did read something about a man just last—

BONNIE
Gilbert Letty. That's why he's in the hospital. He almost died.

CANFIELD
: And before that. Haven't some people—it's been in the papers—

REVEREND BUCKHORN [*soberly*]
: That has been known to happen. We don't deny it.

BONNIE
: They think they have faith. When the test comes, they don't.

COLEMAN
: Why, you're breaking the law. There's a state law against using snakes in church! Daddy, you're just breaking the law every way you turn.

REVEREND BUCKHORN
: State law is not the last word, young Mr. Shedman. The freedom of our religion is not something state governments care to trifle with. We are left alone, most of the time.

COLEMAN
: But it *is* against the law? People *have* died?

REVEREND BUCKHORN [*nods*]
: Yes.

CARL [*troubled by* COLEMAN, *tries to explain*]
: You're confused. You don't understand. When something is real, then something is real. [*Pause*] Like her. See, she was smart as a whip. She was swift as the wind. Always sad when I left her, and happy to see me home again. When she'd hunt, and lose sight of me in heavy brush, she'd jump! jump! as she ran, jump! as she ran, like that. She always found me, too! What does the law have to do with it?

COLEMAN
: I'm confused?

Act II

REVEREND BUCKHORN [*softly*]
Bonnie.

BONNIE [*gently leading* CARL *away from* COLEMAN]
Not now, Carl. Come sit with me.

REVEREND BUCKHORN
But you are right in this, Mr. Shedman. Many question us. Write articles in newspapers. But the truth is, we only do what God plainly told us to do. It is right here in the Bible— [*He reaches out and takes up* NANCY's *Bible.* NANCY, *smiling, deftly removes the letter that was tucked inside its pages*] in the words of the Lord. Yet other churches say it isn't. Why they can't read, I don't know. But we can read. We know what we need, and what we want!

COLEMAN
Yes, and so do I. Here it comes, Canfield, right about now.

REVEREND BUCKHORN
What's that?

COLEMAN
I know what you really want, preacher. And you'll use snakes, elephants, anything that moves, to get it. It is now time, friends, for the holy offering! That's what you want! Gimme, gimme!

NANCY
Oh, Coleman! Don't!

REVEREND BUCKHORN
Are you saying what I think you are saying?

COLEMAN
I sure am. You ain't getting a thin dime out of me, Daddy!

REVEREND BUCKHORN
See that bucket?

COLEMAN
What bucket?

REVEREND BUCKHORN
Way back there against that wall. See it?

COLEMAN
What about it?

REVEREND BUCKHORN
That's our offering plate, in this church. We leave it back there. Nobody even has to look at it, much less put money in it, if they don't want to. We'd rather have no church at all than one built on money.

CONGREGATION
Yes, that's right. Yes!

REVEREND BUCKHORN [*to everyone*]
Go out into the churches of this world! Whose high and mighty preachers say we are crazy. Why, they have people carrying money plates stuffed with dollar bills and pledges and silver, and they stick it right up into God's face, and sing a hymn. It is enough to make you vomit on the cross! [*To* COLEMAN, *mad*] Now, you put your thin dime in that bucket, or don't. In your own kind of talk, we don't give a *flying fuck* what you do with your money! [*Furious,* REVEREND BUCKHORN *checks himself.*] I swore at this man. Not his fault. I lost my temper, curse of my life. Help me, friends. Don't let me sink in the swamps of anger! [*He lets out a tremendous, hair-raising scream.*] OOOOOOOOOOOOOOOOHH-HHHHHHHHHH! *GOD!* OOOOOOOOOOOHHH-HH! *GOD!*

[*He falls to his knees at the altar.* OBY *jumps to his side.*]

Act II

OBY
You all right, Daddy?

[REVEREND BUCKHORN *reaches up for his son's hand.* OBY *grips it hard.*]

REVEREND BUCKHORN
Help me, Son!

OBY
I'm here, Daddy.

REVEREND BUCKHORN
Help me, friends! I'm lost! Lost in anger!

[*He holds out his arms to them, abandoning his service and role of preacher completely. They rush to him, grab his hands, press them hard.*]

Mrs. Wall! Sing something! Help me!

[MRS. WALL *plays "Softly and Tenderly Jesus Is Calling." They all move to the piano and sing, while* NANCY *goes to* COLEMAN.]

CONGREGATION [*singing*]
Softly and tenderly Jesus is calling,
Calling for you and for me;
At the heart's portal He's waiting and watching,
Watching for you and for me.

Come home, come home, ye who are weary,
    come home;
Earnestly, tenderly, Jesus is calling,
Calling, O sinner, come home!

NANCY
See, Coleman! You ain't the only one who gets mad. You ain't the only one who has troubles.

COLEMAN
> Nancy, listen. Come on with me. I'll get you out of this craziness. I want a divorce, but I don't want to leave you in no insane asylum.

NANCY [*in sudden tears*]
> It's you who's in the insane asylum! [*She moves away, hiding her feelings.*]

CONGREGATION [*singing*]
> Oh, for the wonderful love he has promised,
> Promised for you and for me;
> Though we have sinned, He has mercy and pardon,
> Pardon for you and for me.
>
> Come home, come home, ye who are weary,
>   come home;
> Earnestly, tenderly, Jesus is calling,
> Calling, O sinner, come home!

[REVEREND BUCKHORN, *restored, takes over his service again. We can see now, under his calm, he is a fractured man, who must struggle against violent passions.*]

REVEREND BUCKHORN
> Thank you, friends, and praise God. When we ask Him together, He takes away our hate. Don't we know, you can't get rid of it by yourself. It just grows. [*To* COLEMAN, *frankly*] God bless you. If I anger you calling you Son, you anger me calling me Daddy.

COLEMAN
> I won't do it again.

REVEREND BUCKHORN
> Then, brother, let's put it this way. We are both equal creatures of God. You may not like that, and I don't reckon I do, neither, but that's the way God made us. [*He looks at* COLEMAN *differently now, seeing something*

Act II

new in him.] It may seem strange to you, but I've seen you before. Yes, I can see my own eyes, years ago, looking out of your face. But never mind that now. [*To his* CONGREGATION] What do we know about the mysterious ways of God? Nothing. We only seek Him, and we won't get scared by what we find.

CONGREGATION
No, we won't. We won't be afraid. Praise the Lord!

REVEREND BUCKHORN
Now, glory to God! Praise His holy name. So the spirit can move! *Glory* to God!

[MRS. WALL *starts the chord of a hymn, then stops.*]

MRS. WALL
Young man. You, young man.

COLEMAN
You talking to me?

MRS. WALL
Yes, I am. Reverend Buckhorn?

REVEREND BUCKHORN
Go right ahead, Mrs. Wall. Friends, when you have something to say in this church, you say it.

MRS. WALL
You're just the kind of young person that caused me—well, I'm just—oh!

[*She bangs a discordant chord on the piano.* VIRGIL *moves to her, and sits on the piano bench with her.*]

VIRGIL
Can I get you a glass of water?

MRS. WALL
No, Virgil. Thank you. [*To* COLEMAN] Shady Lane Meth-

odist Church gave me a Timex watch and said good-bye. After thirty-one years, I couldn't teach Sunday school anymore. A young preacher who looks something like you did it. He got a girl from the teacher's college. She plays the flute, and makes beads, and talks about children *re*lating to each other, and that's religion now. I was just let loose. I thought I'd die. The only good thing I've ever done in my life was with the Bible, teaching miracles to children. Virgil here was in my class, when he was a little boy.

VIRGIL
Yes, m'am. I sure was.

MRS. WALL
But everybody knows better now. Young man, I got desperate. I couldn't find my religion anywhere. I even went to a baseball stadium, to hear preaching about the Lord. But it was the Lord I wanted, not baseball preaching. All empty smiles, and no power. So then one day, I met Virgil again. He brought me here. To these people you don't think much of. Well, let me tell you, they can keep their powerhouse preachers and baseball religion. Let them play at Sunday school, with flutes and beads and the silly talk of college girls. Because I don't need to teach children miracles anymore. I found the miracles here. I always believed them, and I was right. [*She plays a chord again, feeling better.*] So, you look down your nose all you want to. You bothered me for a minute, but you don't anymore. I'm free of people like you. Glory be to God.

[*While she talks and plays,* LORENA *moves timidly toward the piano.*]

LORENA
Mrs. Wall, that was a thrilling statement.

Act II

MRS. WALL

>Thank you.

LORENA

>I do so enjoy singing with you, and everyone—I—

MRS. WALL

>Thank you, kindly. [*She plays, firmly, and begins singing "I Love to Tell the Story," indicating for* LORENA *to join her.*]
>
>>I love to tell the story of unseen things above,
>>Of Jesus and his glory, of Jesus and his love.
>>I love to tell the story, because I know it's true;
>>It satisfies my longings, as nothing else can do.
>
>[LORENA *joins* MRS. WALL *in a duet.*]

MRS. WALL AND LORENA

>>I love to tell the story; for those who know it best
>>Seem hungering and thirsting to hear it like the rest.
>>And when, in scenes of glory, I sing the new, new song,
>>'Twill be the old, old story, that I have loved so long!
>
>[VIRGIL *joins in singing the refrain.*]

MRS. WALL, LORENA, AND VIRGIL

>>I love to tell the story, 'twill be my theme in glory,
>>To tell the old, old story, of Jesus and his love.
>
>[*When they are finished,* LORENA, *very moved, stands looking at everyone.*]

LORENA

>Oh, I did—I want you to know—I don't know how—

REVEREND BUCKHORN [*gently*]

>Speak, Mrs. Cosburg. We'll listen.

LORENA

>Oh, I can't.

REVEREND BUCKHORN
  In your own good time, then.

LORENA
  But I want to! [*Pause*] They don't know I'm here tonight. My husband, Frank. Or my children. They'll be hurt. They don't understand, like this young man. They make fun of you. I've driven past this church, alone, many times. I never had the courage to come in. I just parked, in the dark, and heard you singing. [*Pause*] My husband tells me what to do. My children tell me what to do. Delivery boys and clerks at the five-and-ten tell me what to do. The only time I ever crossed anybody in my life was coming here tonight. I want to know what you believe. Because in my life—in my own life— [*Wretched, she's unable to go on.*]

REVEREND BUCKHORN
  Gather your forces, Sister Cosburg. Your life is all right. We're not afraid of it, if you're not. Speak when you please. We'll wait.

  [*She nods, grateful, and sits down.* REVEREND BUCKHORN *smiles at her.*]

  You see, we observe no strict order of worship here. Worship don't have much order to it, not if it's real. No preacher can schedule the Holy Ghost, shorely not me. He *will* come, Sister Cosburg, all the same. The answer to that is, wait, and be ready. [*He looks at* NANCY.] As I am ready. For the Holy Ghost. For my little bride, and the joy of our union! As *I* have waited!

COLEMAN
  Hold it. Waited how long? You got a growed-up son. Reverend Daddy. Well, sort of a growed-up son.

NANCY
  Coleman—

Act II

COLEMAN

How did you come by him? Santy Claus? Somebody knit him for you one day?

NANCY

Oh, Reverend! My awful husband! I'm so sorry.

REVEREND BUCKHORN

It's all right.

NANCY

No, sir. It's not.

COLEMAN

Sir? Sir, Nancy? You gonna call him sir when you get it the way you like it, and grab him by the—

NANCY

Throw him out! Throw him out! Just *throw* him *out!*

REVEREND BUCKHORN

Now, hush! [*Pause*] Throw him out? Young man out? Well, I'd like to. He attacks my church, and flaunts his carnal knowledge of my young bride in my face. I must confess, I am tempted. But friend, in forty-three years of Christian ministry, no human soul has ever been cast out of a church by me. [*To* COLEMAN, *boiling*] Of course, there is a first time for everything!

CANFIELD

Come here, son, and sit down, for goodness sake. Nice people and good friends, you see how my client here, he has his problems.

ORIN

He just don't know what they are.

HOWARD

Orin, ain't it the truth?

ORIN
: Yep.

MRS. WALL
: He likes playing bad boy in Sunday school. That's all.

CANCER MAN
: He's a good boy. Strong, and good, inside. I can see that.

CARL [*To* COLEMAN]
: If you could have seen her just once, you'd know what I mean. Thinking about her, you wouldn't get so mad all the time. She was so beautiful. I see her now, all the time, and I don't get so mad anymore. Don't you understand?

BONNIE
: Carl. [*She moves him away from* COLEMAN *gently.*]

OBY
: Daddy?

REVEREND BUCKHORN
: Yes, Son?

OBY
: I need to testify. It's about my new job.

REVEREND BUCKHORN
: Do you have to, right now?

OBY
: I'd like to, yes, sir.

REVEREND BUCKHORN
: Well, all right. Make it short.

OBY
: Friends, I want to tell you something about the religious nature of bowling. I don't know if you've ever seen the quality of hardwood they have now in a first-class bowl-

ing alley. It's beautiful. That clear, pure wood, with the light shining on it, and wonderful empty space, with just the balls rolling down, rolling down. And a clean strike, well, it's heaven. I got a steady job today. *Manager*, now, of the sixteen-lane Bowl-O-Rama Bowling Parlour, off Highway 43, just out of Gardensburg. It's good Christian recreation, for the glory of God and the health of your bodies, and you can get there easy from here. I hope you'll all come, and enjoy it, like I do. Praise God. Thank you, Daddy. [*He sits.*]

REVEREND BUCKHORN
Did you say manager?

OBY
Yes, sir!

REVEREND BUCKHORN
Well, congratulations. But how can you be in church twice a week, too?

OBY
The owners agreed to that. I don't know how to explain it, but they just go together, Jesus and bowling.

COLEMAN [*shaking his head*]
I told you somebody knitted him one day. And that is the man stole my wife for his daddy. You ain't got a momma around for me anywhere, have you?

OBY
Now, don't you talk about my momma!

COLEMAN
Why not? She can't talk for herself, evidently. What happened to her?

OBY
She died.

COLEMAN
Of snakebite, or knitting fatigue?

OBY
Of distemper! When I was the littlest boy. After the other one, and before—

REVEREND BUCKHORN
Son!

OBY
Sir?

REVEREND BUCKHORN
No need to go into all that.

COLEMAN
Whoa! After the *other* one? Other what?

OBY
Wife, of course. Daddy's first. Before my momma.

REVEREND BUCKHORN
Son—

COLEMAN
And when she died, what? How many more?

REVEREND BUCKHORN
There is no need at this time to go into—uh—these—

COLEMAN
Oh, no? Just how many wives you had, Reverend Daddy?

REVEREND BUCKHORN
That is none of your business!

COLEMAN
How many, Nancy? Do you know?

NANCY [*shaken*]
I thought I did.

Act II

COLEMAN
Well, let's see. One before Oby's ma, plus Oby's ma, that's two. One after that, that's three. Three?

[*No answer*]

Four?

[*No answer.* COLEMAN *beams.*]

Five? [COLEMAN *raises his arms.*] Glory to God. *Six?*

REVEREND BUCKHORN [*with dignity*]
Taken by the Lord.

OBY
Except the fifth. She ran off, taken by Satan!

REVEREND BUCKHORN
Hush!

NANCY [*weakly*]
Six?

COLEMAN
Didn't he tell you that?

NANCY
Only about—two.

REVEREND BUCKHORN
I would have, little bride. You know that.

COLEMAN
Sure. In the kitchen, after the wedding, while she's chopping wood, cooking hot bread, and washing babies. [*Pause*] Babies.

OBY [*grinning*]
Been plenty of them.

REVEREND BUCKHORN
Son!

COLEMAN

How many is plenty? How many children you got, Daddy?

REVEREND BUCKHORN

My offspring number seventeen children, thirty-one grandchildren, and—a number of great-grandchildren.

COLEMAN

And six mommas in the cemetery, all wore out. Nancy, I know you wanted babies, but are you ready for this?

REVEREND BUCKHORN

Little bride, you know I will treat you gently.

NANCY [*stunned*]

Six? I'm number seven?

BONNIE

Nancy, never you mind that. He is a good man. Life is hard for women, sometimes, yes. But it is better to marry. It is always better to marry.

NANCY [*hushed*]

But you never did.

BONNIE

Oh. Yes, I did. But it took me too long, you see, to sort out my—carnal nature. I didn't know what I was doing. [*She looks at the rest, and testifies.*] I had it all mixed up with everything else. You see, there was always my sister, Joann. She was the real beauty. Not me. Now, Joann never liked going to church. She said it was dull. So *I* did. I went to church all the time. And if any good Christian boy asked for it, up went my skirts for him every time. I did enjoy it. I always liked an enthusiastic Christian boy. And when Joann would say, "Isn't church dull?" I'd say, "Yes, Joann. Of course, Joann." [*She smiles, and remembers her sister, vividly, dangerously.*]

Yes, Joann. Of course, Joann. [*She looks up again, then goes on brightly.*] But then, Joann got married, to a boy going to be a doctor, and moved away, and there I was, still in church, still giving it out and giving it out, until nobody wanted it. The boys became men, and there I was, still in church, dressed like a little girl, ready to do anything anybody wanted. But the men got tired of me. So, I found me another church, and another, and, sooner or later, every church I joined, I had to leave. Everybody lost their enthusiasm with me, even the plumber-husband I finally got, wherever he is now. And Joann married, her children growing up, telling me not to be such a church-mouse. [*Pause*] Yes, Joann. Of course, Joann. [*Smiles*] Well, I won't tell a lie. I'll still give it away, to a good enthusiastic boy. But I found something better than that, finally. A real church. Stronger than anything. That's what I wanted to tell Joann. What happens here. [*To* NANCY] You're still so young. Marry. [*She turns away.*]

CANFIELD [*jumping up*]
That was deeply moving. I have a daughter I wish had half your sense.

BONNIE
Thank you. What's your daughter's name?

CANFIELD
Hester.

BONNIE
That's a pretty name. Is she a pretty girl?

CANFIELD
She used to be. I used to be a smart looker myself.

BONNIE
I bet you did.

CANFIELD

Then I got my heart condition. Stopped shaving every day, and shining my shoes, after that. One thing led to another. Now I look like this.

BONNIE

You look all right now. You just need sprucing up a little bit. Somebody to wash a shirt for you now and then. Having a heart condition don't mean you can't use it anymore. You can still praise God, and have good times, with new friends.

CANFIELD

I think you're right! Come sit by me.

[*She does.*]

COLEMAN

Canfield, don't forget about my divorce!

CANFIELD

Later. We're in church.

COLEMAN

Church, hell. It's a sideshow! [*To* REVEREND BUCKHORN] When are you going to pull out them snakes?

REVEREND BUCKHORN

That's not for us to say.

COLEMAN

Well, who, then?

REVEREND BUCKHORN

The Holy Ghost, Mr. Shedman.

[*Bothered,* ORIN *gets up and goes to* COLEMAN.]

ORIN

I want to tell this boy. Sonny, what you think you are, you ain't. *I* was that. Ain't that right, Howard?

Act II

HOWARD
> Yep.

ORIN
> And if it hadn't been for this man, and these people, I would have—and I *still* get like that, when I see some young—ah, yet if I couldn't come here, I'd—ah. Howard!
>
> [*He turns to* HOWARD, *who grips him firmly by the shoulders. They embrace.*]

HOWARD
> It's all right, Orin. It ain't going to happen. [*He comforts him. Everybody is respectfully silent, except* COLEMAN.]

COLEMAN [*in a loud whisper*]
> Fags, by God. Queers.

CANFIELD
> Well, son, so what?

COLEMAN
> Well, what are they doing in church? Why ain't they in a bus station somewheres?

CANFIELD [*to* BONNIE]
> What he don't know would fill a book.

BONNIE
> Amen.

CANFIELD
> Lots of men love another man, somewhere along the line. I did, once. It didn't hurt nobody.

COLEMAN
> Canfield? You?

CANFIELD
> Praise God, son. Shut up and listen.

[CARL, *who has been watching* COLEMAN *and trying to explain something to him, now erupts.*]

CARL

Yes, praise God! Praise God! [*He stands shaking, staring at* COLEMAN.]

BONNIE [*softly*]

Oh, Carl.

REVEREND BUCKHORN [*quietly*]

Let him be.

CARL [*to* COLEMAN]

I brought her up. I come to believe there was great blood in her. I trained her. I entered her in the County Puppy Stakes, and she won. Then, in a year, the State-Wide Field Trial. Oh, God, could she hunt. They braced her with a lemon-eyed pointer. Right off, he found a covey. But the quail commenced to walk on him. He didn't know what to do. Like a flash, she run the absolute other way. "What kind of bird dog is that, Carl?" all the rich hunters said—big sportsmen, in their jackets and shiny boots. But I had faith. In just a minute, back she came a-running, having circled them birds in the joy of her smart mind. She boxed them quail in between her and that pointer. The judges said, "She has it, Carl," and I flushed the quail and shot, and got one, and she retrieved it so dainty, set it in my hand with not one feather missing. Looking up into my eyes, saying, Well, Carl, I guess we showed them this time; me saying, Yes, my honey bee, I think we did. Off she run to the hunt again, and she won first place, the blue ribbon and the silver cup, and they poisoned her that night. Fed her ground-up glass in hamburger meat. All night long, she couldn't even lie down. I was on my knees with her, blood pouring out in her piss, her insides sliced to pieces every time she heaved and coughed. My baby. And she died. Why did they do

Act II

that? We never done them hunters no harm, except win one silver cup, just one. [*He stares at* COLEMAN.] I didn't think there could be anything else for me, but her. [*He nods at* COLEMAN.] I filled up with hate. Like you. Orin Hart brought me here. Nothing happened the first time, or the second, or the third. But then, I don't remember just when, I saw her again. She come right in that door, looking for me. And when we pray to God, and the serpents are taken up, she's here. And so I live again, in the blood of Jesus, who conquers hateful men, and gave me back my darling in this church. I praise His name forever. Glory to Him, for His goodness to me. [CARL *stands nodding at* COLEMAN. *There is a pause. Nobody speaks.*] Now I got to go outside, to the bathroom. Excuse me. [*He exits.*]

NANCY

Don't you see, Coleman? Don't you see?

COLEMAN

Yes, I see. And I ask you all, calm and sensible, Is that man crazy, or is he not?

NANCY

Not, Coleman, not!

CANFIELD

Depends, son. Depends.

COLEMAN

He's a lunatic. And you all know it.

CANCER MAN

Son, say you were him. Your dog you loved like that, died like that. What would you do?

COLEMAN

I wouldn't go to Jesus. I'd find out who poisoned my dog, and my daddy and me, we'd break his neck.

CANCER MAN
: I thought you said your father was dead, son.

COLEMAN
: Yes, he is. I mean, *I*'d find out and *I*'d break his neck.

CANCER MAN
: Would that help anybody?

COLEMAN
: Sure. Me.

CANCER MAN
: You just can't get it, can you?

CANFIELD
: Maybe *I* can. [*To* REVEREND BUCKHORN] May I?

REVEREND BUCKHORN
: Yes.

CANFIELD
: Client, the man didn't do what you'd want to do. Does that mean he's crazy?

COLEMAN
: No.

CANFIELD
: He came to church instead. Does that mean he's crazy?

COLEMAN
: No.

CANFIELD
: He believes he found his dog again.

COLEMAN
: *That* means he's crazy!

CANFIELD
: It also means there is maybe one man less in the world with a broken neck! Who's crazy?

Act II

COLEMAN
You are, lawyer, if you think—

CANFIELD
Depends, depends!

[ORIN *moves in on* COLEMAN, *trembling again.*]

ORIN
Broken necks, is it? That what you want?

COLEMAN
Look, don't you mess with me.

REVEREND BUCKHORN
Go ahead, Mr. Hart. Mess with him. What the hell.

ORIN [*pointing at* HOWARD]
See that man? We met fourteen years ago, working the state roads. Mean, both of us. Hung over every morning, standing around the fires, trying to get warm. First time I saw him, I said, "Listen, shrimp, you going to hog all that fire, or am I going to put you in it?"

HOWARD
I said, "Just try it, hog belly. They'll pull us both out."

ORIN
We didn't fight each other. We got drunk that night.

HOWARD
And took on four paratroopers.

ORIN
Howard was already married. I was too, soon after that.

HOWARD
Orin had trouble with May, right off. He wasn't drinking for fun no more. I'd get him home to her.

ORIN
And I did the same for Howard. One time Edna left him,

and took their little girl, Jean, with her. Howard clamped a razor blade in a pair of pliers, and tried to cut his throat.

HOWARD
No, let's skip that, Orin.

ORIN
Razor in one hand, good-bye letter in the other. But he was drunk and crying. All he did was make a mess of his throat. See the scars?

HOWARD
Orin, I said shut up about this!

ORIN
No, Howard, I'm going to tell him. And you ain't going to stop me. Because without me, you'd have died.

HOWARD [*sighs*]
Yep.

ORIN
I was the one who found him, wanting to die, but couldn't. Suicide. I got him to the hospital. I was cool and calm. But in other times, in my domestic torments, sonny boy, it was Howard come to get me, me screaming, wanting to break to pieces any man come near me, and Howard cool and calm, the only man alive could take me home.

HOWARD
Bad ass fighting men. Kill the world.

ORIN
Fighting all the time, since I was a boy. When I had my family around me, and Howard to hold me back, I managed. Then infernal things happened to me.

HOWARD
His boy, Wayne William, got sick and died. His wife

Act II

couldn't stop drinking no more than he could. He was under the wheel.

ORIN

There was a man at the plant named Jackson. He crossed me. I couldn't stop thinking about him. I knowed I was going to kill him.

HOWARD

I knew it, too.

ORIN

I took to hounding the man.

HOWARD

I said, "Orin, don't do it."

ORIN

I said, "You try to stop me, I'll kill you, too." You see, bad ass? What we are from the beginning, it grows in us. It was growing in me. What I wanted all my life. A dead man. I commenced carrying the gun.

HOWARD

I couldn't help him! I didn't know what to do!

ORIN

I showed Jackson the gun. He said, "Why are you doing this to me?" I said, "I don't know. I'm just going to kill you."

HOWARD

I had to do something. I got him drunk that night, and stole his gun. I said, "All right. If it's dead men you want, you'll have two of them. Me and you. Because I can't live without you, Orin."

ORIN

I said, "Why, you fool."

HOWARD

I said, "Move. I heard about a place where crazy people play with death, and rattlesnakes. If that's what you want, we'll do it there."

ORIN

I thought no other man could yell and scream like me. But when the serpents appeared, I'd never seen nothing like it. And the worship. I remembered my wife and children still alive. I thought about all the men I wanted to kill. And I said, "Oh, this torment will end, or I will!" In the music and the singing, I said, "Give it to me! Jesus Christ, you know my evil heart. Give me that snake, you know I want it!" And I took one up. I held my death here, in these hands. And of all the people in the world that night, the Lord anointed Orin Hart.

HOWARD

And Howard Rudd. You see, bad ass?

[*They stare at* COLEMAN, *who stares back, unmoved.*]

COLEMAN

Sure. I see Orin Hart and Howard Rudd. Ain't they pretty?

HOWARD

What the hell you mean?

COLEMAN

I'll tell you. Fruits ain't always like girls. They can look like truck drivers and still be queer, my daddy always said. I don't care about your damn story. You're fags, using a church to fuck each other. It wasn't no Holy Ghost that anointed you, it was—

ORIN [*enraged*]

Son, if you want to get yourself cold-cocked, that man or me, either one—

Act II

COLEMAN [*furious*]
   One at a time, or both together! Come on!

NANCY
   Coleman, don't! Stop him!

REVEREND BUCKHORN
   Let them alone.

   [ORIN *moves slowly toward* COLEMAN. COLEMAN *faces* ORIN *and shoves him.*]

COLEMAN
   Come on, queers! I'll bust open your goddamned—

   [COLEMAN *goes after them, shoving* ORIN *away and knocking* HOWARD *down with a savage elbow to his stomach. Alarmed,* ORIN *rushes to* HOWARD *and bends over him, and* COLEMAN *knocks* ORIN *down.* ORIN *leaps to his feet. With a roar, he falls upon* COLEMAN, *shaking him like a rag doll and throwing him to the floor. Both* ORIN *and* HOWARD *fall on* COLEMAN *and hold him down.*]

ORIN
   Don't mock the Holy Ghost, bad ass!

HOWARD
   Bad ass, when we come in here, we felt the power! Not no foolishness with lead pipes and guns, not no beating and drinking and murder and vice, but the power! I tell you, I seen that roof up there split apart! My mouth dried up. My heart stopped. Down from heaven come the Holy Ghost, and I mean he *moved* on us! *That* was the power! And we loved each other, freely, and said we didn't want to die. Because for the first time in all our miserable lives, we knowed what a victory was!

ORIN
   Saved! *Saved!* Understand, bad ass?

[*They get up, leaving* COLEMAN *on the floor.*]

We had something new to think about.

HOWARD
Glory to God!

[ORIN *stomps his boot down an inch from* COLEMAN's *head. They move away.* NANCY *rushes to* COLEMAN.]

NANCY
Are you all right? Did they hurt you?

COLEMAN [*hurt*]
I'm all right.

[*He gets up.* NANCY *tries to help him.*]

NANCY
Do you need—

COLEMAN [*shakes her off*]
I'm all right!

[*He stands facing them all, but is badly shaken. Enter* CARL.]

So beat me up. I still say this is a sideshow. And I want my legal rights. I won't be put off by lunatics in a circus!

REVEREND BUCKHORN
Friend, we've all lost our tempers with you tonight. We won't do it again. But after what you've heard, how can you call this a circus?

COLEMAN [*almost crying*]
Because you're fakes. My daddy would know. What you do with them snakes is a lie. Unless you want somebody to get bit, and die. You drug them, or something. And then go crazy in here.

Act II

BONNIE [*terribly upset*]
   Want somebody to die? Did you say—

REVEREND BUCKHORN
   Just a minute. [*He takes a faded newspaper clipping from his pocket. He opens it, smoothes it reverently, and shows it to* COLEMAN.] The white-haired man on the floor was named George Hensley. In nineteen hundred and nine, on White Oak Mountain, he was the first to read in the Bible, "They shall take up serpents," and then go out and *do* it. He founded the Dolley Pond Church of God, With Signs Following, in Tennessee. He founded this church, in nineteen forty-eight. Yes, people have died. Laws were passed. And we are still here.

BONNIE
   Oh, God! Don't I know that!

REVEREND BUCKHORN
   Tell him, Bonnie, if you want to!

BONNIE [*moving on* COLEMAN]
   Joann's happiness didn't last. My sister got desperate, too, just like the rest of us. I brought her here. I told her not to move without the power. But she did. She cried out and grabbed a snake and he bit her. She stood right here, his fangs in her arm, hanging from her. She said she'd never go to a hospital. Her faith in Jesus Christ would save her life. She would trust in Him. We prayed with her. She commenced to swell. Her color changed. We made her go to the hospital. But that night, Jesus took her. [*She weeps.*] She's with Him now, in heaven. Awful things were said about me. My own family tried to have me arrested. But I'm still here. I still worship Christ in this church! [*She weeps.*] Some people say I killed my own sister! It's not so! I brought her to God! I brought her to God!

[*She turns to* CANFIELD, *who holds and comforts her.*]

REVEREND BUCKHORN [*moving on* COLEMAN]
We are persecuted. We are against man's law. George Hensley, who led us to his church, finally died, and of snakebite. But he'd been bit and lived over four hundred times! [*Passionately*] You don't believe it? All right, don't! Lots of people like you say we're crazy, to need this worship this strong, this bad! But we do! That is our nature! The Lord Jesus understood us, and in His own sacred word, He told us what to do. [*He points to the altar.*] You see that jar? On the altar, by the cross? That is strychnine poison. If your faith in Jesus Christ is strong enough, you can drink that, and live. That's what the Bible says. You can walk through fire, and not be harmed. That's what the Bible says. You can take up serpents, and not be harmed. That's what the Bible says, and that's what we believe, whether *you* do or not! Stay here, if you want. But don't let me hear you say anything more about a circus! [REVEREND BUCKHORN *mops his brow.*] Mrs. Wall. Give us a hymn, in the name of the Lord. Something quiet. To calm us down. And prepare us for the worship, which I am not holding up no longer. [*To* NANCY, *who is looking at her letter again*] Little bride. I can see you wavering in the faith. Your husband has touched you hard, and filled you with doubt. I never said life with a servant of God is easy. I said it is life. You make up your mind about me and about your husband, and do it now.

[*He turns his back on her and* COLEMAN *and* OBY. *The* CONGREGATION *gathers around* REVEREND BUCKHORN *and* MRS. WALL. *They chat quietly, then sing a gentle hymn.*]

OBY [*to* NANCY]
You're still worried by your husband, aren't you?

Act II

NANCY [*miserable*]
    Yes.

OBY
    Well, talk to him. Maybe you best think again.

    [*He moves away, to the others.* COLEMAN *and* NANCY *are left alone, downstage.*]

COLEMAN
    It wasn't just that night, or that man.

NANCY
    No.

COLEMAN
    When did you decide to leave me?

    [*He moves close to her. She moves back.*]

    I won't touch you.

NANCY
    I decided lots of times. One night, you hit me, and—

COLEMAN
    I'll never do it again.

NANCY
    That's what you said then. And you stuck a little snapshot of me in the frame of that big picture of your momma and daddy and said, "See, I love you."

COLEMAN
    Well, I did.

NANCY
    But I can't live in no picture frame of your momma and daddy! If I'm going to be put in a coffin like that, I want my own children to do it!

COLEMAN
I never said we wouldn't have children.

NANCY
You didn't have to. It was plain enough.

[*Upstage, the* CONGREGATION *sings softly. They sing hymns like "What a Friend We Have in Jesus," and "In the Garden," hymns old, familiar, and quietly passionate, while* COLEMAN *and* NANCY *have it out.*]

COLEMAN
I can see why you left me. I can see why you're here. But this crazy religion is a lie, Nancy. It just ain't true.

NANCY
How can you tell?

COLEMAN
Because I won't lie to myself! With everything else wrong about him, my daddy taught me to see life as it is! And it is mostly god-awful hard! *That's* the truth. Never mind snakes and Jesus. We just have to grow up, and grit our teeth, and face it!

NANCY
Without nothing? No love, no children, nothing?

COLEMAN
We could have that, woman, if you'd just shut up about it!

NANCY
And that your daddy taught you! Shut up, woman! When are you going to learn something for yourself?

COLEMAN
All right. Here I am. There they are. What is wrong about me, without something just as wrong about them?

Act II

NANCY
: You drink whiskey and beer.

COLEMAN
: Yes. But I don't see dead dogs or roofs splitting open.

NANCY
: You curse all the time.

COLEMAN
: Yes. But I don't whine, or cry at you, or beg help from Jesus, like a coward.

NANCY
: You hate me.

COLEMAN
: No, I don't!

NANCY
: And hate yourself!

COLEMAN
: All right. Sometimes. And I work and slave at that miserable fish farm my daddy left me, that I'm scared to leave. I admit that.

NANCY
: And it's work, drink, fish, drink, come home, drink, hit me, drink, and try to make love. That's what you call facing life?

COLEMAN
: It's honest! [*Shaken*] Life is hard!

NANCY
: Too hard for me—with you. It's not that I didn't come to care for you. I did.

COLEMAN
: Do you now?

NANCY [*a great sigh*]
Oh, I don't know. I thought I'd just walk out of my momma and daddy's house and into my husband's house, and have his babies, and it would all be like it was again. And instead of my sisters and brothers and Momma and Daddy, there would be my children and my husband, all around the fire, saying, "We love you, Momma. Welcome home." But what a dream. [*She smiles wanly at him.*] So I picked my husband—you are right about that Sunday school picnic, Coleman—it was a trap I laid for you with my perfume and lace. You walked in it just like a rabbit, and I kicked it shut. But then, my husband was a man with his dreams, too, full of thorns, and so different from mine. So I cried. And this big angel appeared named Oby, and he led me to his daddy, the Reverend Buckhorn, who took me in and made me feel safe, like I was at home, with my daddy, and then happy to be loved, by him, and people and church—[*pause*]—and serpents. So I trusted again. Most of the time. [*Pause*] Six wives? [*Pause*] I've learned a lot. I think.

COLEMAN
Nancy, I got you into this. I'll get you out. You can't marry that old man. You know what he is now. How many times you seen an old buzzard like that, wearing out his wives? He'll work you to death. I can't let that happen to you. Come home.

NANCY
What?

COLEMAN
We'll talk. I promise I'll never hit you again. Never.

NANCY
What about your divorce?

Act II

COLEMAN

We'll talk about it first. Sort it out, like Canfield says. I'll listen to everything you have to say.

NANCY

Coleman, you won't.

COLEMAN

Everything you say. I'll treat you kindly, and gentle. I'll be a good husband. I won't drink. I won't swear. I'll try to quit the fish farm and get another job. What else? I might even take you to church.

NANCY

What?

[*Behind them, the* CONGREGATION *has stopped singing and has been listening to them.*]

COLEMAN

Some decent church. Near home. Hear that? I will! I'll even pray with you. See what I'll do for you? "Praise the Lord. Praise the Lord! Help us poor sinners, O Lord!" See, I can do that. "Praise the Lord! Praise the Lord!"

CONGREGATION

Amen! Amen, brother! Praise the Lord!

[COLEMAN *wheels about. He sees they have all been listening to him.*]

COLEMAN [*enraged*]

What the hell do you mean, listening in on us? I ain't praying in this place! I'm trying to talk to my goddamned stupid wife!

[*And he hits her.* NANCY *sprawls onto the floor, and* COLEMAN *leaps after her.*]

Ah, Nancy!

[NANCY *holds up her hand, keeping both* COLEMAN *and the people away from her.*]

NANCY
See, honey? What would be different? [*She gets up by herself.*] You can have the furniture. I owe you a pickup truck. Good-bye, Coleman.

[*She moves away. She takes out her letter, and looks at it.* COLEMAN *stands shaking.* CARL *approaches him.*]

CARL
Hit me. Make you feel better.

COLEMAN [*choking*]
I don't hit lunatics.

CARL
Just your wife. You think I'm crazy. But I heard you talking about your daddy. I understand.

COLEMAN [*bitterly*]
Oh, yes? Who was yours?

CARL
God is my father. Everybody's here, but yours. He is Jesus's father, too, and His right arm is the Holy Ghost. You're still praying to your mortal father, who's dead. That's bad. [*He holds open his arms.*] I'm crazy. Hit me.

[*The* CONGREGATION *calls* CARL *back.* CANFIELD *approaches* COLEMAN.]

CANFIELD
Your lawyer can't help you. He's converted. To find friends like this at my time of life and in the condition of my heart, is not something I'm going to hesitate about. [*He turns to* BONNIE.] I'm leaving you, client. You can prove desertion now, by your wife *and* your lawyer. I wish—well, good luck.

Act II

[CANCER MAN *approaches* COLEMAN.]

CANCER MAN

They cut me to pieces. I'll be dead, soon, like your daddy, and your mama. That's all right. You don't have to worry about that.

[COLEMAN *breaks. He sobs, grabs a box or a chair, and sobbing, at the same time filled with black rages, smashes it. It is a useless gesture. He kneels amid his little ruin, trembling.*]

REVEREND BUCKHORN

Yes. We wish we could tell you what to do. We can't. We're in this trouble, too, and have to do for ourselves the best we can. [*He turns to the* CONGREGATION.] Preachers talk. What can a preacher tell a soul suffering like that? What can they tell any of us? Nothing. We know it is hopeless. [*He begins his service.*] All we can do is worship. All we can do is turn to the Lord, Who understood us. Because when He rose up into heaven, He spoke, to them who believed in Him, to them He left behind. We turn to those words! What are they, friends? Read me the words of Jesus Christ!

[VIRGIL *goes to the lectern. He reads from a Bible.*]

VIRGIL

The Book of Mark. Chapter 16, verses 17 and 18. "And these signs shall follow them that believe; In my name shall they cast out devils—"

CONGREGATION [*softly*]

Amen.

VIRGIL

"They shall speak with new tongues—"

CONGREGATION [*stronger*]

Amen!

VIRGIL
"They shall take up serpents—"

CONGREGATION
Amen! Glory to God!

VIRGIL
"And if they drink any deadly thing, it shall not hurt them—"

CONGREGATION
No! Never! Amen!

VIRGIL
"They shall lay hands upon the sick—"

CONGREGATION
Amen! Praise God!

VIRGIL
"And they shall recover!"

CONGREGATION
Praise God! Amen! Glory to God! Praise the Lord!

[*From reading the Bible,* VIRGIL, *in a furious rapture, begins to speak in tongues. The strange syllables are pure emotion, erupting from him with great force, twisting his body.*]

VIRGIL
Ah! Ah! Sha—*gon*—du—lah! Sha—*gon*—du—lah! Ma shill—a *hon*—du—lah! Gos—la! Gos—la! [*Possessed,* VIRGIL *speaks in tongues. He goes to the boxes of rattlesnakes, and opens one of them. We hear the snakes rattling.* VIRGIL *takes one out and holds it up.*] Ah—gall—a sonda! Ah—gall—a *sonda!* Eee—ma—nona! Eee—ma—nona! La—gall—*la*—sa! La—gall—*la* sa! [*He puts the snake back, then collapses at* REVEREND BUCKHORN's *feet.*]

Act II

REVEREND BUCKHORN

I remember! I thought I would die. But the heavens came open, and wave after wave of God's love broke over me! I held the serpent, and I spoke in tongues!

[*They embrace.*]

God bless you, Virgil! God bless you, son!

[CANCER MAN *is at the boxes. He takes out a serpent. He holds it up high, and approaches* COLEMAN.]

CANCER MAN

You see! I'm still alive! They said my life was over! But I feel the power of the Lord. I hold the serpent! I defeat him! God gives me this victory! I feel wonderful! [*He holds the serpent out to* COLEMAN.] And see. The snake is calm.

[*He turns, puts it back in the box.* NANCY *moves away from everyone, and reads her letter, thinking hard. The* CONGREGATION *begins to sing "Stand Up, Stand Up for Jesus."*]

CONGREGATION [*singing*]
> Stand up! stand up for Jesus!
> Ye soldiers of the cross;
> Lift high His royal banner,
> It must not suffer loss:
> From vict'ry unto vict'ry,
> In this His glorious day,
> You that are men now serve—

[BILLY *rips out a discordant chord on his guitar and cries out. The singing stops.* BILLY *goes to* COLEMAN.]

BILLY

I didn't start out this way! [*To* COLEMAN] You ain't the only one! [*He clenches his fists in anger.*] I don't want my wife! I don't want my baby! That's the truth! You hear that, Muriel?

MURIEL
Yes. I do.

BILLY
All I meant to do was work in town during the day and play my guitar here at night. That's why I come. Then I met Muriel here. We got in trouble. I did what I thought was right. We got married. But it's not right now! [*He shakes with rage.*] I'm trapped! I can't stand it! Sometimes I hate her! Sometimes I hate—ah, how can I do that! I wouldn't hurt my own child!

[*The* CONGREGATION *moves aside for him. He approaches the boxes.*]

Oh, God, they scare me.

REVEREND BUCKHORN
Billy, you don't reach in every time. You wait for the Lord.

BILLY
I can be free. Lord Jesus, anoint me. Give me the power. [*He takes a deep breath.*] I believe. I'm not afraid. [*A hideous rattle. He takes out a huge rattlesnake. He holds it directly in front of his face.*] Strike. Kill me, if you can. [*He holds the snake, shuddering with terror.*]

CONGREGATION
Praise God! Glory to God, Billy!

BILLY
There! There! Oh, Holy Ghost! [*He puts the snake back in the box, and turns to his wife.*]

MURIEL
God bless you, Billy.

Act II

[*They move aside together, with the baby.* COLEMAN *gets up.*]

COLEMAN
Get out of my way! Get out of my way!

NANCY
No, Coleman! No!

REVEREND BUCKHORN
There's death in that box!

ORIN
You'll risk your life!

HOWARD
You'll put it on the line!

CANCER MAN
If you believe, you'll live!

REVEREND BUCKHORN
But if you don't, you can die! Right here.

[*At the boxes,* COLEMAN *spreads wide his arms.*]

COLEMAN
Stay away from me! I'll do it! [*He reaches down into the boxes. He pulls out two rattlesnakes, and holds them up. He steps forward, staring at them, in stark terror. He turns about, holding them. Convulsions rack him. But when he turns to us again, his face is amazed. He looks up, past the snakes.* COLEMAN *cries out. He is converted.*]

REVEREND BUCKHORN
Praise the Lord! He made us! We are His!

[*The* CONGREGATION *now begins to erupt within themselves. Some are seized by spasms, some shaken by convulsions, some sing, some dance.*]

People say we're crazy! People say Jesus never meant us to *do* what He said! And we say, what do you know about Jesus and His ways! Nothing! Nothing!

[MRS. WALL *has a snake in her hands. She and* BONNIE *face the terrified, but thrilled,* LORENA.]

MRS. WALL
    Sister!

LORENA
    Yes, sister?

MRS. WALL [*to* BONNIE]
    Tell her! Tell her!

BONNIE
    The first time I seen the snakes, I nearly died. I couldn't run. I couldn't move. I stood there, praying. Then the Holy Ghost gave me the power!

LORENA
    What's it like? I want to know!

BONNIE
    Your hands get numb.

LORENA [*eagerly*]
    Yes?

BONNIE
    Then they get cold.

LORENA
    Yes?

BONNIE
    Then they begin to itch!

LORENA
    Oh, *yes!* I never felt like this before!

Act II

MRS. WALL
    Do your hands itch now, sister?

LORENA
    They do!

BONNIE
    Then, if you have the power, grab him.

MRS. WALL
    It's the best feeling you'll ever have!

LORENA
    Give it to me! Give it—

[*They hand her a huge rattlesnake. All three hold it. They scream with pleasure.*]

LORENA, BONNIE, AND MRS. WALL
    Ah! Ah! AHHH! O God in heaven! O God in heaven!

[*Everyone now, except* NANCY, *handles serpents. She sits to one side, with her letter in her hand, silent amid the singing and the shouting. The service reaches its climax. The people move about, stamping and shaking the church. Some cry. Some laugh. Some scream and beat the floor. Some dance. Some sing. Some hold up the jar of poison. Some play with fire. They all release to their Lord the tensions and the sorrows of their lives, moving about as if in some tremendous storm. Slowly, it subsides. Slowly, the snakes are put back in the boxes. The sobbing, the convulsions, the laughter, the singing, and the music stop. They are all exhausted. Silence. Long pause. In a corner, by himself,* CANCER MAN *sags, and kneels.* COLEMAN *kneels by* CANCER MAN. *He grips his hand, hard.*]

COLEMAN
    It's eating on you, ain't it? And them drugs?

[CANCER MAN *nods.*]

I can tell. Hang on to me.

[CANCER MAN *nods.*]

You ever fish?

[CANCER MAN *nods again, surprised.*]

Want to? With me? I know where they're biting.

[CANCER MAN *nods.*]

Then we'll go. Together.

[COLEMAN *stands. He,* NANCY, *and* REVEREND BUCKHORN *look at one another.*]

REVEREND BUCKHORN
Well, young man?

COLEMAN
I want to join the church. Please take me. Don't send me away. [*He sinks to his knees before* REVEREND BUCKHORN.]

REVEREND BUCKHORN
Well, little bride?

NANCY
I'm leaving. [*She holds out her letter.*] They've accepted me, at the business school in town. I'll work for them a while, but make my own living soon. I don't want to be a child no more. And my own babies will just have to wait awhile. [*She kisses* REVEREND BUCKHORN *on the cheek.*] I do thank you. [*She looks at the* CONGREGATION.] I'll come to church again, some day. [*She looks at* COLEMAN, *on his knees. She touches him, gently.*] Good luck, Coleman.

Act II

[*Exit* NANCY. REVEREND BUCKHORN *stares after her, then at* COLEMAN. *He shakes his head.*]

REVEREND BUCKHORN
She goes. You stay. [*Sighs*] Blessed be the name of the Lord.

[COLEMAN *sits and weeps, exhausted. Everybody watches.* MURIEL, *holding her baby, begins to sing, alone.*]

MURIEL [*singing*]
>There's a wideness in God's mercy
>Like the wideness of the sea;
>There is a strangeness to God's blessing,
>Like the thrill of e-ter-ni-ty.

>Jesus defend us, O sweet mercy send us,
>O angels attend us with unchanging love,
>Jesus defend us and sweet mercy send us,
>And angels attend us from heaven above.

Curtain

Picture credits

Page iv, John Wood, photograph by Willoughby Gullachsen, Birmingham Repertory Theatre, Birmingham, England; p. v, Donna Goodnight, photograph by Joe Brannon, East Carolina University Playhouse, Greenville, North Carolina; p. 1, photograph by Ron Jennings, Virginia Museum Theatre, Richmond, Virginia; p. 97, photograph by Conrad Ward, Cubiculo, New York, New York.